T5-CQC-318

# WHY I AM A BAPTIST

# WHY I AM A BAPTIST

Compiled by Joe T. Odle

Broadman Press/Nashville, Tennessee

ISBN: 0-8054-5517-5
4255-17

Library of Congress Catalog Card Number: 71-189504
Dewey Decimal Classification: 286
Printed in the United States of America

*To*

*My Daughter and her family,*

*Sarah, Roland, Melanie and Alan Maddox*

*Dedicated Baptists*

# Contents

**Introduction** 9

**SECTION I. Testimonies: "Why I Am a Baptist."** 13

W. A. Criswell
Billy Graham
Robert G. Lee
Carl Bates
Vance Havner
S. E. Anderson
Landrum P. Leavell II
Wayne E. Ward
T. B. Brown
John R. Bisagno
Noel Smith
Baker J. Cauthen

**SECTION II. Sermons by Representative Baptists: "Why I Am a Baptist."** 41

A Mature Pastor—W. O. Vaught, Jr.
A Young Pastor—Larry G. Rohrman
A Retired Pastor—M. E. Ramay
A Denominational Executive—Paul M. Stevens
A Seminary President—Grady C. Cothen
A Layman—Owen Cooper

**SECTION III. Baptist Distinctives: Joe T. Odle** 85

Baptist Distinctives
The Bible
The Lordship of Jesus Christ
Salvation
The Church
The Ordinances
A Principle
A Program

**SECTION IV. Baptist Devotion to Doctrine and Truth** 115

AMessage by J. D. Grey

# Introduction

The book which you hold in your hands is the result of a command, a concern, an idea, and a conference.

The command is the words of the Scripture in 1 Peter 3:15: "But sanctify the Lord God in your hearts: and be ready always to give an answer to every man that asketh you a reason of the hope that is in you with meekness and fear."

The concern developed when I began to realize through observation and experience that little emphasis is being given to the reasons for the Baptist faith in many pulpits of today and that a large percentage of those in our churches have little real concept of why we are Baptists.

This does not mean that doctrinal position is the only concern I have about needs of modern Christianity or needs in today's churches. I am fully conscious of the tremendous spiritual needs; and I rejoice in the revival which has been manifest among youth, in the spiritual movements among laymen, and in awakening which is being experienced in many churches. I am thankful to God for what he is doing in our midst today and for every organization, group, and individual seeking to do something to meet the spiritual needs. Moreover, I am deeply appreciative of the many books which have been written about this. However, the New Testament reveals that spiritual advance should center in the church and that the church must be faithful to the New Testament in its doctrines and practices. Baptists believe that they are following the New Testament; yet far too many of our members do not know what we believe or why we are Baptists, and little is being written about it. This disturbed me and gave me deep concern.

As a result, the idea developed that there was need for a declaration by outstanding Baptists on why we are Baptists and perhaps a restatement was needed on the distinctives which make us Baptists.

The idea led to a conference with Bill Cannon, one of the editors of Broadman Press, on the possibility of preparing such a book. Cannon suggested that I begin work on the project, since it seemed to be a worthy one.

The first plan was to ask about twenty well-known Southern Baptist leaders to prepare sermon-length messages on the general theme "Why I Am a Baptist." A list of possible contributors was made, and letters went to them inviting participation. As the replies began to come in, it became evident that the plan for the book would have to be changed. Man after man stated that his schedule did not give him the time to prepare for publication a sermon-length message on the subject. Only two or three could prepare what I wanted in the time limit I had set.

A further conference with the Broadman editor brought the book plan to the format in which it now appears.

New invitations for participation were sent out, and I went to work in earnest on the section which called for research of many Baptist books, old and new, to see what men of the past and present have said about Baptists, their doctrines and their history.

Now the book is complete, and it is presented to you.

Here you will find brief statements by well-known Baptists, giving their reasons for being Baptist. Most of them are Southern Baptists, but three other denominational groups are represented. This is a book on why we are Baptists, not on why we are Southern Baptists.

There are six sermon-length messages on the same theme by representative men. Each man represents a different area of Baptist life.

The compiler and editor uses almost one-third of the book to summarize what he found in searching through many books which Baptists have written about their distinctives and their history.

Finally, an outstanding pastor, who has served more than one-third of a century in a strategic pulpit in a great city, but who also has been very active in denominational life and in the work of Baptist World Alliance, writes on the devotion to truth which makes Baptists what they are today.

My personal testimony as to why I am a Baptist is not included in the book. I, too, could tell of the background of a Baptist family and especially of a young pastor who took special interest in the youth of his church. I also could tell of other influences which have touched my life along the way. Nevertheless, my real reasons for being a Baptist are found in the summary on Baptist distinctives found in Section III of the book. These are the things I believe. This is why I am a Baptist.

I make no claim that the book represents all facets of Baptist thinking nor that it represents the thinking of every member of the Baptist family. The fact is that no one Baptist can speak authoritatively for all others or for even one other.

Neither do I claim that the men whose testimonies are found here are representative of all Baptist positions since no effort was made to choose writers representing widely varying points of view. Rather, I simply put down the names of some men I knew who are Baptist by conviction, and who do not hesitate to say so, and I asked them to share their testimony in this book.

The book is very frankly conservative in its theological stance, since this is the position of the compiler and, I am convinced, of the majority of Baptists. However, I most certainly acknowledge that not all Baptists are conservative.

The book is not a theological treatise on Baptist doctrine, searching out the depths of meaning which the theologian must pursue. This book is written for the average Baptist, not for the theologian.

The book makes no effort to present arguments on why a person should be a Baptist rather than a member of some other denomination. Baptists hold convictions which make them what they are, but they have not set themselves up as judges of others. They consider as a Christian every person who accepts Jesus Christ as Savior and Lord and will always walk with him and work with him in kingdom affairs so long as New Testament principles do not have to be abandoned or sacrificed.

Contributors simply were asked to write on "Why I Am a Baptist." Their messages are published exactly as they were received, except that in a few cases some paragraphs were deleted because of space limitations.

This, then, is a book by some Baptists about why they are Baptists. It is hoped that it may help other Baptists to come to a deeper understanding and conviction concerning their faith.

It also is hoped that it will help those who are not Baptists to better understand why Baptists are what they are.

Finally, the book is sent forth with the prayer that God will be glorified by the testimony which is found in its pages.

If these things are accomplished the purpose of the compiler and authors will have been fulfilled.

JOE T. ODLE

# SECTION I

## Testimonies

## "WHY I AM A BAPTIST"

## WHY I AM A BAPTIST
### W. A. Criswell

(Dr. W. A. Criswell is pastor of First Baptist Church, Dallas, Texas. He is a former president of the Southern Baptist Convention and is the author of many books. He is considered by many to be one of the outstanding Baptists in the world today.)

If I can be absolutely and perfectly honest in answering the question, "Why Am I a Baptist?" I would write the reply in two parts. Let me attempt to do so now.

In the first place, why I am a Baptist would concern those early years that brought to me my conversion experience, my baptism, and my church membership. I grew up in a little town, in a little white, cracker-box church house. It was a Baptist church and my people had been Baptist people for generations before me. I hardly knew that any kind of a faith existed other than that represented by our precious church. I went to Sunday School as a boy and I was trained there as a teen-ager. I grew to know the meaning of Jesus for my life through those godly people there and in the ministry of our consecrated pastors.

It is most patent, therefore, that I became a Baptist because of my parents, my upbringing, my early teaching, and the church influences that surrounded the first years of my life.

The other part of the answer lies in an altogether different world. Why do I stay a Baptist? Why do I not join the Catholics? or the Mormons? or the Christian Scientists? or any other one of the 257 differing denominations that make up the religious life of America? The sure reply to this proposition would contain a whole volume, and I am sure that herein is found the reason for the publication of this splendid book by Dr. Joe Odle. As you read these pages, you see why we continue to be Baptists. At the risk of being redundant and superfluous, let me summarize a few things that hold me forever to the Baptist faith and message.

I continue to be a Baptist because the message I deliver from the Bible fits precisely our Baptist conviction, faith, and practice. I never have to apologize for being a member of our dear church when I open that blessed Book and seek to tell the people exactly what God has said. I would be most uncomfortable, for example, standing in a Pedo-Baptist pulpit and preaching from the third chapter of Matthew, the eight chapter of Acts, and the sixth chapter of Romans. Belonging to the faith that I do, I preach these chapters and all the rest like it with heavenly ease and deepening conviction.

Remaining a Baptist, I find myself in an ecclesiastical atmosphere that is not only true to the New Testament but one that also blesses my own heart and spirit. I am free in my work, in my pulpit ministry, and in the explanation of my convictions. I am completely, absolutely, everlastingly free. There is no bishop, there is no hierarchy, there is no machine, there is no overlording ecclesiastical authority to tell me when, where, what, how, and anything else. I can be myself, truly and really, being a Baptist. I love this. I am dedicated to this. I would have it no other way.

So much more could be said and ought to be said, but this is enough for now. One could easily see from reading these words that in my deepest soul I love being a Baptist.

## WHY I AM A BAPTIST
**Billy Graham**

(Dr. Billy Graham is the most widely known Baptist in the world today. He probably has preached to more people than any other preacher in history. While in his evangelistic programs he works with Christians of all denominations, he is a Baptist and is a member of First Baptist Church, Dallas.)

I have never once regretted my decision to unite with that segment of Christ's church called Baptist. The reasons are found in

Baptist convictions with which I share.

In my ministry of the past twenty-five years I have had wonderful fellowship with believers of many denominations. I feel almost as much at home in evangelical churches of other denominations as I do with evangelical Baptists. My own wife is a Presbyterian. Some of my children are Baptist and some are Presbyterian. It has been my privilege to move in circles that have brought me into contact with leaders of practically all denominations throughout the world. Some of God's greatest saints are by conviction members of other denominations. In a sense my ministry belongs to all of God's people whatever their religious affiliation, nationality, language, or color of skin. The whole world of Christian faith has been my parish.

However, my church affiliation is Baptist and I share with Baptists certain basic convictions:

*First,* I am a Baptist because Baptists take the Word of God, the Bible, as their supreme authority in all matters of faith and practice. Most Baptist services center around the Word of God and the proclamation of its truths. As has been said, they have "no creed but Christ, no law but love, and no book but the Bible." Their creed, their discipline, their rules of faith and practice have historically been the Bible.

*Second,* Baptists advocate baptism for believers only. They hold that if baptism is the badge or mark of the Christian and if a Christian is one in whom faith has been awakened, then baptism, rightly administered, must be for believers only. No responsible Baptist would claim that baptism is necessary for salvation, but it is essential if we are to be obedient to our Lord in following his example and instruction.

*Thirdly,* I share with Baptists a strong belief in the priesthood of believers. Baptists believe that a church is composed only of those who have been gathered by Christ and who have placed their trust in him. Thus all are equal, all may pray, witness, and serve. The minister is the chosen leader but each member, being a believer, is equal in status.

*Fourthly,* I share with Baptists a conviction that the New Testament teaches the independence of the local congregation. Membership in a Baptist association or convention is only for fellowship, combining our energies in service, and sharing common interests. Each church, Baptists teach, is a divinely appointed unit, functioning to glorify Christ and to win people to him.

*Fifthly,* I share with Baptists a strong belief in the separation of church and state. Baptists have scrupulously avoided political entanglements and crippling alliances. Baptists were in the forefront for religious freedom, both in Europe and America, and they have played an important part in the guarantees embodied in the First Amendment of the American Constitution.

But most of all, as an evangelist, I share with Baptists their strong emphasis on evangelism and missions. Wherever I go throughout the world, I can always count on the Baptists assisting and supporting my efforts to win the lost.

Lloyd Douglas, the famous novelist, coined a phrase which aptly describes millions of Baptists—"a magnificent obsession." I believe that Baptists, more than any other major evangelical segment of the church, have an obsession to get the gospel to as many people as possible while there is time.

The people of Jesus' day accused him of "being beside himself" and they accused Paul of being "mad." When Baptists declare Jesus Christ and him crucified as an answer to the frustration, problems, and dilemmas of the world, we too are accused of being mad. After watching one of our crusade telecasts in New York, a columnist in that city wrote in his column, "Billy Graham is beside himself." He could have paid me no greater compliment! He went on to say that it is foolish, even ridiculous, to suggest that the answer to the world's problems lies in the cross of Christ. Without realizing it the columnist was using almost the identical words of the apostle Paul. For centuries Baptists have been "beside themselves" with enthusiasm, vision, passion, and faith.

It is my prayer that Baptists will always keep this strong emphasis on evangelism and missions. The world appreciates and understands enthusiasm until it becomes religious fervor; then immediately enthusiasm becomes suspect. You can be as mad as you like about sports, pleasure, money, or drink. You can be mad about a pop star and still be considered a sane and normal person. But bring that same enthusiasm into evangelism and we are accused of being "beside ourselves." Yet hundreds of thousands of Baptists are dedicated to Christ and must of necessity be possessed of that fervor to bring to others the message of the gospel which he or she has experienced.

Baptists have been able to maintain the zeal of their early founders. Baptists have carried the plain truths of the gospel around the world, reckoning nothing of peril or reproach. They surmounted obstacles, overcame difficulties, and endured persecution. That has been their madness—the madness of doing great things for God. I share that madness with them!

## WHY I AM A BAPTIST
**Robert G. Lee**

(Dr. Robert G. Lee is pastor emeritus of Bellevue Baptist Church, a former president of the Southern Baptist Convention, author of many books, and considered by many to be one of the greatest preachers of the twentieth century.)

There are a few reasons I shall give.

I was

*1. Brought Up.*

Yes, I was reared to be a Baptist. My father, though not an educated man, and my mother, who was not an educated woman —as we speak of education today—these two brought me up under Baptist influences in a Baptist church and in a Baptist home.

Once, when I attended a Presbyterian church one Sunday—when there were no worship services at the little Baptist church where my mother's membership was—there was the christening of a little baby by the Presbyterian pastor.

After we left the church house and were on the way home, in a horse-drawn, one-seated buggy, my mother said: "Bob, that baby christening is not baptism as the Bible teaches baptism."

And my father, whose brother Charlie was a Methodist, said, as to the question of falling from grace: "When God saved you, he saved you forever." He believed and taught me that anybody who is really born again from above can never be unborn from below. He detested the teaching that asserts that baptism of the body saves the soul. He said once: "If baptism in water is necessary for the forgiveness of sins, then the blood of Jesus does not cleanse from sin—as the Bible says."

Yes, I am a Baptist.

I was Baptist born.

I was Baptist bred.

And when I die, I will be a Baptist dead.

Yes, by a consecrated Baptist mother, born again by the Word of God and the Holy Spirit, by a determined, doctrinally sound father, who got his convictions mostly from the Bible which he sometimes called "The Baptist Book"—I was brought up. And that is one strong reason why, many years after the death of both, I am a Baptist.

Then, too, I am a Baptist because of

*2. Selective Comparisons.*

In the years of my young manhood, with a burning desire to be a preacher, I heard a number of preachers—some Presbyterian, some Methodist, some Campbellite, and one of the Nazarene belief. Along with these I heard some evangelists in tent and tabernacle meetings—Baptists, Methodist, Presbyterians—all fervent and earnest.

The Presbyterian advocated infant baptism. This I could not accept. The Methodist asserted that a man could be saved and then lost. This I did not believe—and, when I became a preacher, I could not declare.

The Campbellite declared that a person had to be baptized to secure forgiveness of sins and salvation. This I rejected, for I read in the Bible: "The blood of Jesus Christ cleanseth us from all unrighteousness."

In my mind I "sorted out" what these preachers believed and preached. I decided that my convictions as to some doctrines would not permit me to be other than a Baptist preacher.

Moreover, I am a Baptist because of the influence on my mind and life of the

*3. Convictions of Some Baptist Scholars and Statesmen.*

The principles they believed and preachingly and printedly propagated, by pulpit and press, were—and are: (1) The Bible is the final authority in all matters of faith and practice. (2) Each individual is to come directly to God for himself. (3) Salvation is by faith alone without human merit or works of any kind. (4) Scriptural baptism is the immersion in water of believers only. (5) A church is a local, self-governing, independent, democratic body of baptized believers. (6) There should be religious liberty for all people. (7) There should be complete separation of church and state at all times—no matter what, no matter who, no matter where.

I am a Baptist because of

*4. Baptist Beliefs.*

Being a Baptist really means to hold certain beliefs. Somebody said: "When you become a Baptist, you don't just join a church, you join a cause." Here are the beliefs I learned and have and hold today:

In the rights of the individual—no close ecclesiastical rights.

In personal faith, not proxy faith.

In the priesthood of all believers, not the priesthood of a class.

In free grace, not sacramental grace.

In the direct approach to God, not the indirect.

In the believer's baptism, not infant baptism.

In the voluntary principle, not the coercive principle in religion.

In the unity, sufficiency, and sole authority of the Scriptures as the rule both of doctrine and polity.

In credible evidence of regeneration and conversion as prerequisite to church membership.

In immersion only, as answering to Christ's command of baptism and to the symbolic meaning of the ordinance.

In the order of the ordinances, baptism and the Lord's Supper, as of divine appointment as well as the ordinances themselves.

In the right of each member of the church to a voice in its government and discipline.

In each church, while holding fellowship with other churches, solely responsible to Jesus Christ.

In the freedom of the individual conscience and the total independence of church and state.

That in religion we have no priest but Christ.

That in sin there is no sacrifice but Calvary.

That in all things we have no authority but the Bible.

That there is only one confessional and that confessional is the throne of grace.

For these beliefs our Baptist forefathers, who wrote history in blood before they wrote it in ink, lived and sacrificed and died.

## WHY I AM A BAPTIST
### Carl Bates

(Dr. Carl Bates is pastor of First Baptist Church, Charlotte, North Carolina, and president of the Southern Baptist Convention 1970, 1971.)

I am not aware of all the reasons, after all these years, of really why I am a Baptist. To be sure, there are reasons. I list below a few of these.

First, I am a Baptist only by the grace of God. I was a member of another denomination until I was nineteen years old. My mother and father were both dedicated members of our church. I united with that church at age twelve. Upon being asked by its pastor if "I did not think it was time I joined the church," my reply was that if he thought I should, then I would do so.

Several years later I was convicted of my lost condition and committed to our heavenly Father what was left of my life, with no known reservation. I went home to my pastor to tell him that I had been "saved" and that I believed God was calling me to preach. I needed encouragement and careful counsel but received neither.

I went to see the Baptist pastor (Charlie Thompson of Liberty, Mississippi) and he took time to hear my conversion and call-experience and gave me the encouragement and guidance I needed at that moment. I made my profession of faith and was baptized by another Baptist pastor (Dr. J. B. Quinn of Summit, Mississippi) and was licensed by that church.

Mississippi Baptists provided an opportunity for immediate Christian training in Mississippi College. Southern Baptists made it possible for me to attend Southern Seminary in Louisville, Kentucky. Various Baptist churches have permitted me to serve with them across the years.

I did not become a Baptist by conviction but I have remained one by conviction. I am convinced that Baptists have offered me my finest opportunity to respond to the call of God to preach the gospel. Their belief in a regenerated church membership has permitted me to work with believers indwelt by the same Holy Spirit who inspired the Holy Scriptures and blesses with authority the preaching of the truth revealed therein. Baptists have given me a free pulpit in an autonomous church that believes not only that no hierarchy should interfere in a local church but that neither should the government. Baptists have respected the competency of my soul in my spiritual pilgrimage and have provided me a broad platform from which to share spiritual insight with all mankind. These are some of the reasons I am a Baptist.

## WHY I AM A BAPTIST
### Vance Havner

(Dr. Vance Havner is a widely known Southern Baptist evangelist and Bible teacher. The author of numerous books, his home is in North Carolina.)

I have good fellowship with all who know and love the Lord, but I am a Baptist because I believe that the basic and original Baptist position is that of the New Testament church. I do not accept all that some Baptists believe nor do I endorse all that some Baptists do, but I stand on what Baptists started out to believe and do. Some Baptists have departed so far from this position that they would not be recognizable as Baptists to their forbearers. One old giant of my earlier days whom I came to know and admire used to say, "When some of these Baptists get right they'll be with me for I'm where they used to be!"

Dr. George McDaniel defined a Christian as one who accepts Jesus Christ as his Savior, submits to him as his Lord and takes the New Testament for the law of his life. I believe that is a good definition of a Baptist. Anything less is inadequate. Anything more is superfluous.

I remember another Baptist preacher who was converted from a different faith. When asked how it happened, he said: "It was just plain carelessness. Somebody left a New Testament lying open and I read it." I believe that anybody who gets hold of a New Testament, reads it, and obeys it is very likely to come out of that experience a Baptist.

## WHY I AM A BAPTIST
### S. E. Anderson

(Dr. S. E. Anderson is a former member of the faculty of Northern Baptist Theological Seminary, Chicago; member of faculty of Judson College, Elgin, Illinois; pastor; Bible teacher; author; and member of an American Baptist Convention church.)

I am a Baptist because this name, with its beliefs, is endorsed by the New Testament.

*1. John the Baptist was divinely approved.*

God prepared a Baptist preacher, John the Baptist, to start his new work in the world, four hundred years after Malachi. This great man of prophecy (Isa. 40:3–5; Mal. 3:1; 4:5) pioneered the New Testament era (Matt. 11:13; Mark 1:1–11; Luke 16:16; John 1:6,33; Acts 10:37; 13:24).

Christ endorsed the message and baptism of this first Baptist (Matt. 3:13–17). He praised John profusely and frequently (Luke 7:24–30; John 5:33–35).

The Holy Spirit filled John the Baptist even before his birth (Luke 1:15). Therefore, the message and baptism of John had divine authority equal to that of any other New Testament preacher (Matt. 21:23–27).

Since I want to honor and obey the Father, Son, and Holy Spirit I accept John the Baptist as the official Forerunner of the New Testament.

*2. John the Baptist introduced New Testament doctrines.*

(1) John was the first to declare the deity of Christ (John 1:34, 36).

(2) He first preached the substitutionary atonement (John 1:29).

(3) He taught the preexistence of Christ (John 1:15,30).

(4) He said much about the Holy Spirit (Matt. 3:11; Acts 11:16).

(5) He declared the kingdom of heaven at hand (Matt. 3:2; Luke 16:16).

(6) He preached repentance, meaning through conversion (Matt. 3:2).

(7) He insisted on confession of sin before baptism (Matt. 3:6).

(8) He taught immersion-baptism of believers, thus death-burial-resurrection of Christ for us (John 1:31). His baptism pictured the entire gospel (1 Cor. 15:1–4). The Holy Spirit records his "baptizing" as describing his entire work (John 1:25–26,28,31; 3:23; 10:40; Acts 10:37; 13:24). The same is true of Christ's work

(John 3:22,26; 4:1,2).

(9) John taught certain judgment on unsaved sinners (Matt. 3:7, 12).

(10) He insisted on individual responsibility (Matt. 3:9; Luke 3:10–14).

(11) He exemplified genuine humility (John 1:15,23; 3:27–30). No Baptist should boast except in the cross of Christ (Gal. 6:14).

(12) John preached the real New Testament gospel (Luke 3:18), the same evangel as all the later New Testament preachers. "And many other things in his exhortation preached (*euaggelizeto,* Greek) he unto the people."

*3. The name "Baptist" is important.*

The name "Baptist" is found fifteen times in the New Testament, always with real honor and meaning.

This name is descriptive of the best Christian (Matt. 11:11 where the word "least" should be "later," referring to Christ himself).

This name was approved by Christ and the apostles.

The name suggests the gospel in its condensed form (1 Cor. 15:1–4).

Since John the Baptist evangelized and baptized the twelve, they were then Baptistic in beliefs and practice (John 1:35–45; Acts 1:21–22).

The twelve, with Christ, preached the same Baptistic gospel (John 4:1–2).

Their multitudes of converts, therefore, had Baptistic beliefs and Baptist baptism (Acts 2:41–47).

This Baptistic gospel and Baptist baptism continued except for heresies springing up like weeds. One such was the false "baptism" of the men in Ephesus (Acts 19:1–7) who *thought* they had John's baptism. But they knew nothing of the Holy Spirit whom John preached; they were removed by twenty-five years and six hundred miles from John and were likely not even converted until they met Paul.

In the New Testament there was no need, as now, for denominational names. But since the believers were Baptistic they could have been called Baptists.

*4. Good Baptist churches are most biblical.*

(1) We have the same gospel as given by John the Baptist and Christ.

(2) We have the same baptism as endorsed by all the New Testament.

(3) We hold the same doctrines as given in the entire New Testament.

(4) We have similar church democracy and polity as then.

(5) We have the same liberty from dictators as then.

(6) We have the same freedom from Old Testament laws and ordinances.

(7) We have similar church leaders as then—pastors and deacons.

(8) We have similar evangelism, missions, and teaching ministries.

(9) We have the descriptive name that Christ honored so greatly.

How could I, or Baptist churches, be more biblical?

## WHY I AM A BAPTIST
**Landrum P. Leavell, II**

(Dr. Landrum P. Leavell is pastor of First Baptist Church, Wichita Falls, Texas; president Texas Baptist Convention; former president, Southern Baptist Pastors Conference; Bible teacher, and evangelist.)

This subject implies that, at the very minimum, some consideration has been given to this matter. Indeed it has! There have been times without number when I have been forced to "look to the rock from whence we were hewn."

At the very outset I must confess that the name Baptist is not as important as the name Christian. Belonging to a denomination can in no way be compared to belonging to Christ. When one has found Christ as personal Savior, it does then become important that he find a medium through which to express that faith. I am a Baptist because of

*Inheritance*

My parents, grandparents, and other forbearers on both sides of my family have lived for Christ in the Baptist fellowship. My paternal grandparents, who lived in Mississippi, made a substantial contribution to the growth and development of Baptist life. My maternal grandparents, who lived in Maryland and came over from Wales, were leaders in the Baptist church in their community. My father and his eight brothers, who were blessed with above average intelligence, were committed to Baptist beliefs and position. All of this contributed to my being a Baptist, but it was not the only or the final influence. I am a Baptist because of

*Integrity*

My conscience will allow me to do no less than to serve Christ through the Baptist fellowship. I have studied the stance of other denominations from the time I was a teen-ager. This continuing investigation has made me aware of the position, both historically and doctrinally, of other Christian groups. I remain a Baptist, understanding the position of other denominations, because I am convicted that we are closer to a New Testament church than any other. Should God give me any other conviction than this, I would pray for enough integrity to unite with the group I believed to be closer to the teachings of Jesus Christ. I am a Baptist because of

*Incentive*

The incentive which impels me is the constant emphasis on reaching human beings for Jesus Christ. Southern Baptists have grown strong on a steady diet of evangelism. No other denomination can match the record of ours in this emphasis across many years. God has blessed every effort we have put forth to reach people. I count it a privilege to be a part of a Christian fellowship which gives priority to winning people to Christ.

Another incentive which constantly challenges me is the Southern Baptist emphasis on missions. While we are concerned for the lost at home, we are continuously faced with the need of a lost world. There is enough challenge for any sincere, growing Christian in our ranks. I am both proud and unashamed to be a part of this Christian fellowship.

## WHY I AM A BAPTIST
**Wayne E. Ward**

(Dr. Wayne E. Ward is professor of Christian Theology, Southern Baptist Theological Seminary and an author.)

I am a Baptist today for one very simple reason—I am deeply convinced that in their basic beliefs and in their church polity Baptists are following the New Testament teachings more closely than any other Christian denomination. Like all Christian groups, our actual attainment falls short of the New Testament ideals which we profess. But it is all-important that we be heading in the right direction and that we have a freedom in our church structure and in our individual Christian lives to allow the continuing reexamination of all our doctrines and practice in the light of the New Testament.

Baptists have always allowed me this freedom and have encouraged me to "search the Scriptures" and be guided by the truth of Jesus Christ which I find revealed there. If Baptists ever forsake the authority of Jesus Christ as revealed in Holy Scripture and try to impose some other creed or authority, I will be compelled by conscience to leave them. Or, rather, I would consider that Baptists had forsaken their basic tenet and repudiated their own essential nature—a fellowship of Christian believers who have freely responded to the call of God in Jesus Christ and committed themselves to obey his teachings, as revealed in Holy Scripture and interpreted by the Holy Spirit within the community of faith. If

Baptists ever deny me this freedom of conscience under the authority of Scripture, I will search for another group of Christians which does preserve this freedom and authority; and I will join them. If I cannot find such a group, I will do my best to call together such a fellowship in Jesus' name, under the guidance of his Word, and in the presence of his Holy Spirit. The long centuries of Christian history are filled with the sad story of church authorities who tried to impose creeds and doctrines upon their members and others, forcing those who sought the freedom and authority of Christ in his Word to "come out and be separate." Baptists have always been those who had no ecclesiastical head but Christ, no creed but the Bible, no way of salvation but by personal faith in the Lord Jesus Christ, and no baptism but believer's baptism to show forth the believer's identification with the death and resurrection of Jesus Christ. With an overwhelming sense of joy I give myself to the fellowship of those people who proclaim and practice these New Testament teachings.

There is no doubt that parents and family have a great deal to do with determining the denominational choice of the child or young person. But it is also just as true that the influence of parents cannot perpetuate a denominational tradition which the children do not come to believe in themselves. My parents were both Methodists until some time after my oldest brother was born. Both my father and my mother had grown up in a rural community where there was just one church, the old Gravel Hill Methodist Protestant Church. Born in the Kentucky revival movement of the nineteenth century, this church preached salvation by grace through faith, the necessity of the new birth, and believer's baptism by immersion. As teen-agers, both of them had been converted and baptized by immersion in an Arkansas pond. When they married they moved to town and joined the First Methodist Church. The young Methodist preacher insisted that their first son be "baptized" immediately, as an infant. They were horrified. Dad insisted that he must make that decision for himself when he was old enough. "You sound like Baptists," the young preacher replied. And indeed they did. Not long after, they were baptized into the fellowship of the First Baptist Church. Throughout the following years, they had the joy of seeing their first son, and all the rest of us in turn, make a personal profession of faith in Christ and follow him in baptism. Like my parents, I would not hesitate to leave any church which denied the teachings of the New Testament, as I understand them, and find a church which would give to me and to all others the freedom to follow the truth of Christ as revealed in the Bible.

Paul summarized in forceful words the essential characteristics of the New Testament church in Ephesians 4:5:

1. *One Lord.*—Jesus Christ alone is Lord over his church. No bishop or pope can usurp this place of authority over the church, because Christ is alive and present in his church and guides it by his Spirit.

2. *One faith.*—Personal trust in Jesus Christ as Lord and Savior is the only kind of faith the New Testament knows anything about. Such concepts as "latent faith" in infants (Martin Luther) and "vicarious faith" on the part of parents or godparents (Reformed theology) are completely foreign and contradictory to the biblical concept of faith.

3. *One baptism.*—Buried with Christ by baptism into his death and raised to walk in a new life (Rom. 6:4) is the only form and meaning of Christian baptism which is taught in the New Testament.

I am a Baptist because I have found these essential characteristics of the New Testament church both taught and practiced in Baptist churches.

## WHY I AM A BAPTIST
### T. B. Brown

(Dr. T. B. Brown is pastor of the Mt. Helm Baptist Church, Jackson, Mississippi, a church which cooperates with the National Baptist Convention, Incorporated. He also is president of the Mississippi Baptist Seminary.)

There is a well-known proverb in Baptist circles that says: "If a black person is not a Baptist, some white person has been dictating his religion."

My family dictated the religion of my childhood. My father was a Missionary Baptist pastor for fifty-six years in Mississippi.

My father's religion was a religion of simplicity and so was his preaching. He believed all the Bible to be the word of God. Its warnings deeply moved his soul. Its promises were his comfort and strength. My father believed God heard his prayers and would answer them. He spent long hours on his knees in prayer. The family altar was an established institution in our home; my father led the family in prayer.

He believed in a salvation that delivered from all sin. His life was sincere and transparent before God and man. He always had a clear and definite testimony and was never ashamed to give it. His faith in God gave him victory over sin and temptation. The world had lost its charm for him. He was in the world but not of the world. He had peace and poise in the midst of the most adverse circumstances. He was a great believer in Romans 8:28: "And we know that all things work together for good to them that love God, to them who are the called according to His purpose." When everything else failed him, these words held him steady on course.

Worship for my father was very simple also. The house of worship did not have to be colorful and costly. Stained-glass windows and tall spires neither attracted to nor detracted from his preaching. Well-trained choirs and thundering organs were not necessary to his worship. The mission hall or the humble home was a sanctuary, as well as the big, new church building, when God was there.

Formal ritual and studied order of service affected him no more than the free and spontaneous service. His religion was based upon his love for his Savior and the conscious reality of God's presence whatever his surroundings.

My father was a radiantly happy Christian. He did not endure his religion—he enjoyed it.

Why am I a Baptist? After my father led me to accept Christ as my Savior and Lord, I wanted to be the same kind of Christian my father was.

Now, after thirty-one years in the ministry, I find that my convictions concerning the Baptist position are just as strong as were my father's, so that I am what I am not only because of what he taught me but because of my own study of the Bible and of Baptists and their doctrines.

This is why I am a Baptist—a Baptist preacher.

## WHY I AM A BAPTIST
**John R. Bisagno**

(Dr. John R. Bisagno is pastor of First Baptist Church, Houston, Texas, and is one of the outstanding younger preachers in the Southern Baptist Convention. His churches have led the Convention in baptisms for several years. He is the author of several books.)

To be perfectly frank, I became a Baptist because my parents were Baptists. I was saved at a Baptist encampment and was educated in a Baptist college. But the fact that I have stayed a Baptist through the years has probably no relationship to either of the foregoing facts. I shall, however, in these brief sentences resist the temptation to write of the usual great doctrines that we as Baptists hold dear, such as the separation of church and state, priesthood of believers, and so forth. There are some other things that mean much to me personally about the people called "Baptists."

Baptists are true to the Word of God and are narrow in the

important things without being so narrow-minded as to exclude the man who may differ on secondary issues. For example, salvation is by the grace of God reflected in Christ, reconciling the world to himself; the Bible is the inspired word of God; and Jesus died for our sins and rose according to the Scriptures. These are truths from which I believe Baptists will never sway.

There are other issues, probably not quite as important as these, on which we disagree with others and yet can be agreeable in spite of our differences: such matters as open and closed communion; the three millennial viewpoints; even speaking in tongues and eternal victory. If the truth were known, there are many issues on which some people in many Baptist churches disagree; and yet one can be a Baptist and not hold the same viewpoint of his fellow church members on these issues. It might amaze you some Sunday to take a survey of your people and find how many members really do not believe in "once saved, always saved." And yet we do not dismiss the membership of anyone who shall disagree with us.

Some churches greatly err in refusing fellowship from persons who do not practice the church covenant as regards the partaking of alcoholic beverages, while the same churches overlook that part of the covenant which forbids gossip, talebearing, and backbiting. This ought not to be. I am grateful, however, that with Baptists this is the exception rather than the rule, and men are free to find their own approach to God as long as it is through the shed blood of Christ, and are free to worship and live, according to the dictates of their own hearts, in light of the Scriptures as they understand them.

I am a Baptist because Baptists are evangelistic in nature. In my opinion, Jesus sent the sinner word on the needs of social ramification of the gospel when he said, "What shall it benefit a man if he gains the whole world, and loses his own soul?" Our own church has a strong social ministry, but it will always remain secondary to the prime task of winning men to Christ. Missions and evangelism are the dual edge of the cutting point that have made Baptists great. Evangelism must have an educational program to give support and direction to a new Christian. We have a well-regulated, formulated basis for our evangelism. With this, Baptists are primarily an evangelistic, outreaching, world-vision-centered denomination. Personally, this is my life style. If it were not so of my denomination, I could not be a Baptist.

Lastly, I am a Baptist because Baptists are controlled by the grass roots of the Bible. No hierarchy dictates church views on doctrines. Any Baptist church is free to do anything it votes to do any time it wants to do so.

One or two rioters can give an entire city a bad name; a few teens can place a blight on all teen-agers. It is also true that far too many times those in high places who err from the faith give our denomination the tremors and make us think that Baptists are down the pike, gone down the tube; but such is not the case. It is my opinion that no man or group of men in any place of leadership will ever sway from the grass roots of our doctrine. Our doctrines and our faith are not in the hands of people; they are in the hands of God. I feel that most of our people have put God first. I believe in our people. I believe in our future. I believe in Baptists.

## WHY I AM A BAPTIST
### Noel Smith

(Dr. Noel Smith is editor, Baptist Bible Tribune, Springfield, Missouri, publication of the Bible Baptist Fellowship, International.)

Here are a few of the reasons why, in the midst of the dissolution of the basic institutions of civilization, being a Baptist increasingly gives me a feeling of spiritual and intellectual anchorage.

Baptists are a people. They have an historical identity. They have an historical image. Their continuity is the longest of any Christian group on earth. Their doctrines, principles, and practices are rooted in the apostolic age.

I am not a Pharisaical sectarian. But I don't confuse Baptists with the Reformation, with the Reformers. The Reformers wanted to reform the Roman Catholic Church; the Baptists were against the church. Because it was not a New Testament church, Protestantism originated in the Reformation. Protestantism is protest—ism. That's negative. Negativism has within it the seed of its own disintegration.

The Baptists were not reformers. They were not protestors. They were positive.

Freedom of conscience is not a Reformation doctrine; it is a Baptist doctrine.

The separation of church and state is not a Reformation doctrine; it is a Baptist doctrine.

Religious liberty is not a Reformation doctrine; it is a Baptist doctrine.

Believer's baptism is not a Reformation doctrine; it is a Baptist doctrine.

Baptism of the believer by immersion in water, symbolizing the believer's death, burial, and resurrection *with* Christ, is not a Reformation doctrine; it is a Baptist doctrine.

The local, visible, autonomous assembly, with Christ as its only head and the Bible as its sole rule of faith and practice, is not a Reformation doctrine; it is a Baptist doctrine.

Worldwide missions is not a Reformation doctrine; it is a Baptist doctrine. The Reformers had no missionary vision and no missionary spirit. For almost two hundred years after the Reformers, the Reformation churches felt no burden to implement the Great Commission.

What kind of a world would the Western world have been had Protestantism become its master?

Who but the Baptists kept Protestantism from becoming its master?

The general attitude today is that truth is determined by the passing of time; that there are no eternal, abiding truths. "You can't turn the clock back. Time invalidates all truths. Time invalidates one set of truths and fastens another set upon us."

Baptist history repudiates this philosophy of fatalism. Baptists today are believing, teaching, preaching, and practicing the truths that were believed, taught, preached, and practiced two thousand years ago.

It gives me a feeling of stability to reflect that I, as a Baptist, am in the stream of this long continuity of faith and practice.

The Baptist people are a great continuity. They are a great essence. They are a great dignity.

The world never needed them more than it needs them today.

## WHY I AM A BAPTIST
**Baker J. Cauthen**

(Dr. Baker James Cauthen is best known as a missionary statesman and executive secretary of the largest Baptist mission board in the world, the Foreign Mission Board of the Southern Baptist Convention. He was a pastor, a seminary professor, and a missionary before coming to his present position.)

I grew up in a Baptist home. My father was a deacon, and my mother was a teacher of an adult Sunday School class for many years. When I was a baby, she pushed me in a baby buggy in parading, along with many other Christian ladies, through the streets of our town in an effort to drive out liquor. They were so successful that to this day, it has never been able to return.

When I was six years old, I came to feel my need of a Savior, and along with my brother, who was three years older, made a profession of faith in Christ, and was baptized. About two years later there began to grow in my heart a deep feeling of God's call to his service. It settled upon me with solid conviction, and determined the course for all the years to follow.

Just before my seventeenth birthday, when I was a freshman in college, a country church with fifty members invited me to become pastor. While feeling my inability, I saw no reason why I should not accept this call to duty, and begin the ministry that was so deeply implanted in my heart. My father and my mother were so supportive of my efforts that I felt the undergirding of their prayers and confidence.

My Baptist convictions grew through study and experience in country churches, evangelistic meetings, college, university, and seminary studies, followed by a delightful pastorate of a city church, and teaching experience in theological seminary.

What I saw in the study of the Scriptures and came to understand through deeper insights into theology were reinforced by observations growing out of church history and practical experience in the work of the ministry.

I came to see Baptist churches as groups of believers in Jesus Christ who had followed our Lord in baptism and were united in covenant relationship to share the gospel of Christ with all the world. It seemed to me their strength lay in fidelity to the Scriptures, reliance upon a living Lord, and yieldedness to the guidance of the Holy Spirit. The autonomy of local churches linked with a beautiful sense of cooperation growing out of common convictions of truth and a sense of purpose born of the Great Commission, seemed to me to be the secret of power and effectiveness.

I came to see that the greatest bonds of unity are not ecclesiastical structures holding domain over individuals and churches by means of overriding authority but a common conviction of the truth of the gospel and a great sense of missions under the guidance of the Holy Spirit.

Particularly, as I have seen on mission fields throughout the world the gospel making its way in other lands, have I been grateful for the basic concepts which characterize Baptist life. A New Testament church is the same wherever you find it, because it is made up of believing people who have responded to Jesus Christ in discipleship. They are responsible to our sovereign Lord and are bound to one another in ties of love and cooperative action for the sake of evangelization of the whole world. They are at home in any land and form their own associations and conventions to project work as they feel God leads. Their autonomy growing out of a sense of a direct responsibility to the Lord Jesus Christ, is matched by a sense of cooperation and fellowship born of a deep sense of purpose and mission. They carry a note of hope to the individual man causing him to feel his dignity as a child of God through faith in Jesus Christ and his responsibility to relate to all his brethren in order to serve effectively the Savior who died for all the world.

I have been a Baptist minister for forty-five years and have preached the wonderful gospel of the Lord Jesus throughout the world. It has been my joy to share in the life of churches, associations, and conventions throughout this country and throughout the world. I am fully convinced that Baptists are a people whom God can wonderfully use if we will stay true to his word, be zealous for his worldwide mission, and yield ourselves completely to the guidance of the Holy Spirit. All this is possible while holding deep in our hearts affection for all our fellow Christians, of whatever group they may be, and with minds so deeply convinced of the truth of the living God, that we look with eagerness and expectation upon all of the advance of learning in whatever field, knowing that the truth can only reflect the glory of God and assist us to deeper understanding of the Scriptures which are the record of God's revelation of himself through Jesus Christ, our Savior and Lord.

# SECTION II

## Sermons by Representative Baptists

## "WHY I AM A BAPTIST"

*A Mature Pastor*

## WHY I AM A BAPTIST
### W. O. Vaught, Jr.

(W. O. Vaught, Jr. has been pastor for twenty-seven years of Emmanuel Baptist Church, Little Rock, Arkansas.)

No man can divorce himself from his background and from the influence of his parents. My parents were Baptists and therefore I became a Baptist. To be sure there is more to the story, but that is where the story begins. A tall young theologian by the name of E. Y. Mullins had just become the pastor of the Harrodsburg Baptist Church in Harrodsburg, Kentucky. He engaged a country boy in conversation one day and asked him if he were a Christian. The country boy told him that he was not but that he wanted to be. The conversation caused that boy to realize his need for a Savior, and as a result, he was converted, and Dr. Mullins baptized the new convert in the Salt River near Harrodsburg.

In another section of Kentucky a young woman, reared in a devoted Christian home, joined the Baptist church in Springfield, Kentucky, and began to walk the Christian path. After being graduated from college, the boy from Harrodsburg and the girl from Springfield met, fell in love, and were married. On their honeymoon trip to Niagara Falls, the young bride packed a white Bible in the top of her suitcase, and on the first night of their married life, they began their lifelong habit of reading the Bible and praying together before going to bed.

Returning to Kentucky following their honeymoon, this young couple began their married life by affiliating with the Baptist church. It was into this home my sister and I were born and early came to feel the deep Christian convictions of these devoted parents.

My father was a schoolteacher and along with his duties as principal of the school in Versailles, Kentucky, he and my mother were active in the Baptist church. The first photograph I have of our family was made in the Sunday School room at the old Versailles Baptist Church, and here my sister and I took our first steps in the Christian life. Early we both became professing Christians, following in the steps of our parents.

Early in our youth my family moved from Kentucky to Mississippi, and one night in a "protracted" revival meeting in Brooksville, Mississippi, my sister and I made our public profession of faith and joined the little Baptist church. Dr. Zeno Wall was the revival preacher and Rev. Owen Williams was the pastor. Therefore, I must say that I am a Baptist because of my home.

Quite often I have wondered why I was converted at such an early age. I joined the church at eight years of age, but I had been a professing Christian in my heart long before that. I also knew long before that time that I would become a Baptist preacher. In fact, no other great ambition ever swept through my mind. I think I didn't understand my early conversion until the day my father died in Nashville, Tennessee. I was standing by his bed, watching him breathe his last struggling breath, and the thought came to my mind that I became a Christian not from anything my father had taught me, but rather from the things I "caught" both from my father and my mother. I saw Christianity lived in a modest and humble home. I saw the love of a great father for a great mother, I saw the meaning of daily Bible reading and prayer, and I "caught" an atmosphere of Christlike living that just can't be put into words. Therefore, I must conclude that I became a Christian and a Baptist because of a home.

I do not wish to leave the impression that my father and mother did not teach us Baptist doctrine. Indeed they did, and early in my life I came to know the content of Baptist doctrine. I learned the meaning of salvation by grace through faith, and I early came to realize that church membership was for baptized believers only. I learned that the Bible was given by inspiration from God and is the only guide for Christian faith and conduct. My parents discussed these great Christian doctrines in my home and I remember how my heart would burn and my young mind would reach out for these great truths with eagerness and satisfaction.

In the second place, I am a Baptist because of Baptist schools. When I was a tiny boy, the great professors from the Southern Baptist Seminary often visited my home in Versailles, Kentucky. They would be on their way for their preaching appointments in that section of Kentucky, and they made our home their stopping place. I would sit close beside them and listen to Dr. Mullins or Dr. Sampey or Dr. Robertson talk about the great theological school in Louisville. My heart would burn within me, and it was then that I decided as a three-year-old that I would one day go to that school to "learn" how to be a Baptist preacher.

All of my grade- and high-school life was spent in Mississippi, and when I was graduated from high school in Caledonia, Mississippi, I turned my face toward Mississippi College. I really never had any other thought than that I would attend a Baptist college. At Mississippi College I found my place in the Baptist Student Union and in the college Baptist church. I took part in all student religious activities, but the deepest impression that was made on me came from the influence and example of those great professors who taught us and lived their Christianity before us. No one could watch men like "Zeus" Latimer and "Dutchy" Provine and "Tite" Wallace and not be a better Christian.

At Mississippi College for the first time I began to see the great depth of the Baptist faith. I also came to get a glimpse of the worldwide program of missions. From Mississippi College I journeyed for my first time to Ridgecrest, North Carolina, and met the Baptist student leaders from across the nation. Here I heard the great spiritual leaders like Dr. Charles Maddry, Dr. George

W. Truett, Dr. Louie D. Newton, Dr. M. E. Dodd, Mr. S. D. Gordon, and many others. I fell in love with the Baptist program and decided that I would devote my life and energy within the framework of this denomination.

At this point I might add that I am a denominationalist. I have never had any temptation to shed my denominational loyalities for a wider ecumenicalism. I have found perfect liberty in the Baptist faith, and I believe I gained this insight through Baptist schools.

After four years at Mississippi College, I turned my face toward the Southern Baptist Seminary at Lousiville, Kentucky. Just a few years prior to my attendance at the Southern Seminary, the campus has been moved from downtown Louisville to the beautiful new campus called "The Beeches." Here I met Dr. John R. Sampey, affectionately known as "Tiglath." I sat under the teaching of Dr. Sampey and Dr. Robertson and Dr. Dobbins and Dr. Carver. I was blessed by close fellowship with fellow-students from across the nation who made up that student body. There has not been one day in my ministry since my seminary days that I have not had some occasion to use the things that were taught me by those godly men. Their teaching was true to the Word of God, and if I ever accomplish any worthwhile things in my ministry, much of the credit is due these men.

In the third place, I am a Baptist because of a Book. The doctrine of the Bible is the only Baptist doctrine we know. Baptist doctrine and Bible doctrine are one and the same. We believe we should let the Bible speak for itself and we do not have a right to speak on matters of doctrine apart from the teaching of Scripture.

The first doctrine I mention, and the one that is most precious to me is this—*Salvation by grace through faith.* This is the doctrine of all doctrines. We are not saved by what we do, but by what he did for us on that "old rugged cross." Salvation is not an achievement, but an acceptance. Indeed we can do nothing to assist in our salvation, for Christ has already done it all. Riding my black pony on that Mississippi farm, I often sang "Jesus paid it all, All to Him

I owe." I believe this is the greatest doctrine of Christianity.

The second doctrine I mention centers around the Bible's answer to the question, *Who is God?* I find ten essential qualities given in the Bible in answer to this question. They are as follows: sovereignty, justice, righteousness, eternal life, love, omniscience, omnipotence, omnipresence, immutability, and veracity. I believe God has these qualities, Christ has these qualities, and the Holy Spirit has these qualities. From this I conclude that God is one in essence but three in personality.

The third great and precious doctrine to me is the *infallibility of the Scriptures.* Let me sum it up under a paragraph called:

## THE ORIGIN OF THE BIBLE

"Knowing this first, that no prophecy of the scripture is of any private interpretation" (2 Pet. 1:20). The word *"is"* comes from *ginomai* which means "originate." The word *"private"* comes from *idios* which means "from one's very own." Thus, the literal reading of this Scripture should go like this: "Knowing this first, that no prophecy of the scripture originated in anyone's own private thinking."

"For the prophecy came not in old time by the will of man: but holy men of God spake as they were moved by the Holy Ghost" (2 Pet. 1:21). Let us read it literally—"For this prophecy came not in old time by the will of man: but holy men of God spake as they were picked up and carried along by the Holy Spirit."

Let us sum it up this way: The Scripture in the Bible did not originate in the minds of men. God so directed the writing of Scripture that without waiving their human intelligence, their individuality, their literary style, their personal feeling, or any other factor, his complete coherent message to man was recorded with perfect accuracy, the very words of the Scripture bearing the authority of divine authorship.

* * *

Baptists hold that God has given to each of us the right to interpret the Scriptures for himself. Scripture is the perfect truth of God, and the more we know the Scripture the more we know the thinking of God. Indeed 1 Corinthians 2:16 concludes that the Bible is the mind of Christ.

I am a Baptist because I believe every man is responsible to God and to God alone. I believe that every individual must believe for himself, be baptized for himself, and answer to God for himself. This causes me to believe in the doctrine that each church is independent and free and each church should be made up of regenerated members.

I am a Baptist because I believe in the separation of church and state. Again and again in the Word of God I find the clear teaching that no state should ever lay its hand on the life of the church and the church should never dictate policy to the state. Greatest freedom has come to mankind under this system. Baptists indeed believe in a free church in a free state.

These are some of the reasons why I am a Baptist. But let me conclude these paragraphs by stating that though I am a Baptist, I believe I am a brother to every redeemed man on the earth. Every man who has put his faith in Jesus Christ is a part of the body of Christ, and is therefore my brother beloved.

*A Young Pastor*

## WHY I AM A BAPTIST
**Larry G. Rohrman**

(Larry G. Rohrman is pastor of First Baptist Church, Jackson, Mississippi.)

Perhaps you have heard of the Baptist pastor who asked his neighbor why he was a member of the Methodist Church. The neighbor explained: "Well, my father was a Methodist, my grandfather was a Methodist, so I'm a Methodist." The Baptist pastor, trying to show what he thought to be an error in logic, questioned his neighbor further. "Tell me sir, if your father had been an idiot and your grandfather had been an idiot, what would you have been?" "I guess I would have been a Baptist," replied the neighbor.

That amusing story does raise a pertinent question. Why am I a Baptist? My convictions are so strong about this matter that I was overjoyed to have the privilege of sharing them with others through this book. I feel as though I have a unique position because of an unusual background. Since that is true, I must start developing my case with my life history.

Neither of my parents are church attenders. When I was young, my father was asked often to sing in the Lutheran Church in our hometown. When I was born, I, like my brother and sister, followed the normal and expected procedure of being taken to the church as infants for baptism. I have deep respect for the Lutheran Church and particularly for their emphasis upon catechism. Unfortunately for me, my brother and sister got a much better foundation of Bible knowledge than did I because we moved before I was old enough to receive much of the teaching from the Lutheran Church.

The move I just mentioned located my family across the street from my paternal grandparents. They were very devout Christians and very regular in attendance at their church which was an interdenominational congregation. As best I remember the church, and I must admit my memories of those years are fading, there was a very heavy emphasis upon emotion. The ministers there were very itinerant, lacking in theological training, and very graphic in their picture language, particularly when describing the second coming of Christ and hell. Very often I saw the pastor display extreme emotion. I witnessed speaking in tongues regularly, and shouting "amen" was an outward expression of an inner spiritual feeling and was not spared or discouraged.

It was during this period of my life that I came face to face with Christ. I recognized the fact that I was a sinner, realized that the only hope of my redemption was in my acceptance through faith the salvation offered to me because of the love and mercy of God. I became a Christian, walked down a sawdust trail under a tent on Highway 83 between Pharr and McAllen, Texas. There has never been a doubt in my mind concerning that life-changing decision. I have been a child of the King since that day.

However, I began almost at once to have difficult problems with the "organized church." I began to ask questions about my new-found faith. In some instances I got no answers to my questions and in other instances I got answers that I could not accept or believe. The truth of the matter is, I had become a Christian because I was afraid not to become a Christian. I was very much afraid of God. Fear was, without question, my primary motivation for striving to live like a Christian. I was so afraid that Christ would "come back," as the traveling preachers put it, and would catch me doing something wrong. Later in life I was able to find that although fear is an acceptable motivation for serving God, there is a much higher motivation. The day I began living as a Christian because I loved God was the greatest day of my Christian life. Let me hasten to say that though love is now the motivation for my Christian life, I have never lost my fear of God and hope I never do. (It is actually reverential awe and not fear.)

Lest I be misunderstood concerning my remarks about the years of my life spent in the Pentecostal environment, I wish to make several comments. Just as I have deep respect for the Lutheran Church, I have profound respect for the Pentecostal Church. I came in contact with some of the greatest Christians it has been my pleasure of knowing during these years of my life. Those people were not only completely serious about their relationship to Christ, they were uncompromisingly dedicated to the task of living for him. Their emphasis upon holiness is very healthy unless it leads to self-righteousness or Pharisaical legalism. And I also wish to say that to subtract emotion from religion is insanity and to discourage emotion in worship is an attempt to confine the Holy Spirit.

One of the gravest mistakes made by the "more sophisticated" churches is to create an atmosphere in which the Holy Spirit is not welcome unless he makes his appearance when it is scheduled on the order of service. (And that, by the way, has to be at the printer's office by Wednesday at noon.) I almost get angry when words like "Holy Roller," "Pentecostals," and other labels are used with obvious negative overtones. (If I may offer a word of advice to the reader, this is it. Never, never criticize another person's method of worship. That is sacred to all men. His way is as right to him as yours is to you.) I also believe that if the Lutherans, Presbyterians, Methodists, Baptists, and so forth, could agree on their theology and let their worship be tempered by the emotion of the Pentecostals based upon the Holy Spirit's presence, we would really have something.

Now, I'm finally down to my assigned subject, "Why I am a Baptist." It is very simple. I am a Baptist because I believe the Baptist faith is the closest church to the New Testament of any church I know. Furthermore, if I find a church closer to the New Testament (at all points) I'll join it. Let me explain that!

There are several reasons, from a doctrinal viewpoint, that are the real factors in my deciding to be a Baptist. The first of these is baptism. However, baptism was the stumbling block that kept me out of the Baptist church for several years. I had been sprinkled in the Lutheran Church and immersed in the creek by a Pentecostal preacher. Now what more could one ask? I was informed however, that I could not be a Baptist without being immersed in a Baptist church. I came to several erroneous conclusions concerning this matter. I thought at first I was being told I couldn't be a Christian without being a Baptist. My second conclusion was that the Baptists didn't think my baptism was as good as theirs. I then thought they were being very narrow-minded, bigoted, and authoritarian. I thought perhaps they want to add me to their statistical table by reporting me as a "convert." Finally I realized that none of these assumptions were correct.

Baptists believe that baptism should be administered to believers only and should be by immersion only. The reasons for believing that baptism should be by immersion are three: (1) We believe that the baptism experiences in the New Testament were by immersion. This is clearly seen in Matthew 3:16, where the Bible states: "And Jesus, when he was baptized, went up straightway *out of the water.*" Again, in Acts 8:38–39: "And he commanded the chariot to stand still: and they went *down both into the water,* both Philip and the eunuch; and he baptized him. And when they were *come up out of the water,* the Spirit of the Lord caught away Philip. . . ." Baptists seek to emulate the life of Christ and follow the teachings of the Bible as closely as possible. Therefore, we believe baptism should be administered as it was in New Testament times. (2) The New Testament word for baptism is *baptizo* which literally means "to immerse" or "to put under." (3) Baptists believe baptism is symbolic of death, burial, and resurrection. It is symbolic of the death of Christ, his burial, and his resurrection. It is symbolic of our physical death, our burial, and our resurrection. But, most significantly, it is symbolic of our death to a life of sin, the burial of that life, and the spiritual resurrection of the Christian to a new life.

Because of this final reason, baptism has no particular meaning to a person who has not experienced salvation by receiving Jesus Christ through faith. Again, look at Acts 8:36–38: "And as they went on their way, they came unto a certain water: and the eunuch said, See, here is water; what doth hinder me to be baptized? And Philip said, *If thou believest* with all thine heart, thou mayest. And he answered and said, I believe that Jesus Christ is the Son of God. And he commanded the chariot to stand still: and they went down both into the water, both Philip and the eunuch; and he baptized him." Philip said you must first believe. Infant baptism has no scriptural basis. It can mean nothing more than a dedication of a child to the Lord. Baptists have no argument with the practice of dedicating a child to the Lord, but they don't call it baptism. They call it dedication. Baptism is an outward picture of an inward experience. In picture language one says to those present: "I have died to an old life and it is buried; I am now resurrected to walk in the new life given me by Christ Jesus." Baptism has nothing to do with salvation. Salvation is that which qualifies a man to be baptized.

A question often asked is, Why do Baptists not accept the baptism of other churches? Although there are several answers to that question, the one that satisfies me most is that the person wishing to join a Baptist church must wish to do so badly enough to submit to the doctrinal beliefs of the church. If not, he should be a member of another church with which he can agree. If Baptists received members of any other church without asking them to be baptized, they would, of necessity, be forced to receive members from all churches without baptism. Because of the divergence of belief about baptism they would create a theological state of confusion. One year the children in the church could be taught by a former member of the Church of Christ who would inform them that they have to be baptized to be saved and the next year they could be told by one who holds the Baptist position that they do not have to be baptized to be saved. Baptists are saying, "If you wish to be a member of our church, you must submit totally to our theology." This is at least one point at which the person is requested to submit to the church. Baptism is not an obligation, it is an opportunity. One has the privilege of communicating the gospel in picture language to any person present. It identifies one with a movement. This is the exact reason Christ was baptized. Baptism, for him, was not to wash away his sin—he had committed no sin. My baptism in the Baptist church is a beautiful memory in my Christian experience.

The second significant doctrinal belief that makes it absolutely necessary for me to be a Baptist is the priesthood of the believer. The Baptist church is a noncreedal church. There is no authority in a Baptist church except the Bible itself. However, the Baptist church recognizes the fact that the Scripture must be interpreted. In some other denominations the tradition of the church dictates the doctrinal stand. That is to say, what the church has traditionally believed through the ages is the stand of the church. One of the serious difficulties of this position is that the tradition keeps changing. The hierarchy keeps changing its mind about what the church believes. When a change is made, the person in a local church is informed of the change and is thereby expected to adjust his doctrinal position accordingly.

In still other religious groups the doctrinal position is set forth in a creed written by men and taught to the members of the local church. However, since the creed is simply a statement of doctrinal belief and since it is written by human beings, it needs revision, updating, and correction. In final analysis the creed is little more than a human interpretation of God's word. Humans are always fallible.

No hierarchy can ever tell an individual Baptist what to believe. No creed will ever be handed an individual Baptist for the purpose of dictating his theological position. Baptists believe no man or group of men are infallible. The doctrine of the priesthood of the believer simply means every believer in Jesus Christ who has had a regeneration experience is qualified to interpret the Scripture for himself while being led by the Holy Spirit. Thus there are Baptists who disagree doctrinally with other Baptists. This is one of the strongest points for the Baptist faith. It permits an open-minded search of the Scripture by every person. It is an encouragement to every person to develop his own faith by the constant study of the Bible. It allows room for growth. My theology means more to me now because I have studied through the Bible myself. No one else told me what to believe. It is very hard to live by another man's faith. Baptists are those who decide to remain agreeable while in the midst of disagreement.

A further reason for me to be a Baptist is the form of church government. Each local church is an autonomous group to itself. No other group anywhere tells it what to do or believe. The local church owns its own property, calls its own pastor, and manages its own affairs. Each local church strives to emulate the New Testament as closely as possible. Other denominational groups are in the process right now of discovering just how important this matter is. A movement to develop one gigantic church by joining all denominations is underway. There is only one way that this can be accomplished—compromise. Baptists will never do this. We believe what we believe and cannot change our beliefs. If the Bible says it, it is settled. Many local churches of other denominations are being told of changes that will take place. Much to their chagrin they are discovering there is very little they can do except leave the denomination and the local church because they do not own the property, the denomination does. This could never happen in a Baptist church. A local Baptist church voluntarily cooperates with the association (group of local Baptist churches), state convention, and Southern Baptist Convention. But no authority is vested in any group except the local church.

These are the significant reasons that I am a Baptist. Although the Baptist church is a noncreedal church, there are some Baptist distinctives. That is to say that these doctrinal beliefs are held by all Baptists. Some of these individual beliefs are agreed to by other denominations but when all eight of these things are present in the doctrinal position of a church, it is for all practical purposes a Baptist church or its exact copy. However, other groups add to these eight doctrinal positions and in so doing usually become something other than Baptist in their beliefs. These distinctives are as follows:

(1) Baptists believe in the absolute authority of the Scripture as the only accurate source of revelation upon which is based the faith and practice of the church.

(2) Baptists believe in baptism of believers only, by immersion only.

(3) Baptists believe in complete religious liberty. This includes the right to believe as well as the right to disbelieve. It also demands the complete separation of church and state.

(4) Baptists believe in congregational church government as opposed to the hierarchical system or a representative type of church government.

(5) Baptists believe in the priesthood of the believer. Stated otherwise, they believe in the competence of every soul before God. Every Christian can and must go before God for himself and needs no mediator other than Christ.

(6) Baptists believe in the symbolic view of the ordinances. In the Baptist faith there are two ordinances: baptism and the Lord's Supper.

(7) Baptists believe in simplicity in worship as opposed to liturgical worship. Their worship is midway between the liturgy of the Catholic Church and the free worship of the Pentecostals. It is orderly enough to insure dignity and reverence but spontaneous enough to include congregational participation.

(8) Baptists believe in the lordship of Christ. This is the unifying distinctive.

Although this is not an all-inclusive list of Baptist beliefs, it enables one to determine what makes Baptists distinctive from other religious groups. I believe each of these statements and that is why I am a Baptist.

In addition to these theological reasons, a few concluding statements should be made. Baptists are true to the Bible. They are growing rapidly which seems to show God's favor with them. They are evangelical as was the first-century church described in Acts. It is a missionary-minded church which seeks to share the gospel with every man everywhere and it is doing so with great success. The Baptist church provides an environment in which my spiritual needs can be met in my worship, service, and witness.

*A Retired Pastor*

## WHY I AM A BAPTIST
**M. E. Ramay**

(M. E. Ramay is pastor emeritus, First Baptist Church, Edmond, Oklahoma.)

Practically every New Testament reference which has anything to say about the church, including: its founder, its head, its constitution, and its doctrines could be used as a text or proof text on this subject. We shall use or refer to many of them in the course of our study.

The *Handbook of Denominations in the United States* (published by Abingdon Press in 1961), Frank Mead, lists a total of 254 religious bodies with a total of 314,345 churches reporting a total membership of 112,226,905. In the book the author gives a brief history of each group reporting, with the basic doctrines of each. The beliefs or doctrines vary widely. As I consider these numerous opinions or beliefs, plus a score of other differences, what can I say as to why I am a Baptist?

### I. The Bible, the Word of God

I am a Baptist because I believe the Bible is the Holy Spirit inspired, infallible, unchanging, and unchangeable word of God.

"All scripture is given by inspiration of God, and is profitable for doctrine, for reproof, for correction, for instruction in righteousness" (2 Tim. 3:16). (See also: Isa. 40:8; Deut. 4:2; Rev. 22:18, 19.)

When we want to know what God has to say about man: his origin, his nature, and his destiny; when we want to know what he has to say about sin, salvation, joy, suffering, or happiness, we do not go to creeds, articles of faith or confessions of faith, but we go to the Bible. The question for a Baptist is, what do the Scriptures say?

John F. Sullivan speaking for the Catholic Church in his book,

*The Eternals of the Catholic Faith,* said, "Our church holds and always has held that the sacred Scriptures are the written word of God. In the words of the council, she belives and teaches concerning the books of the Old and New Testaments, that God is the author of each and believing this, she also believes that the Scriptures can contain nothing but perfect truth in faith and morals. But if this be so, does it follow that God's word would be contained only in them? By no means! Our church affirms that there is an unwritten word of God also which we call 'apostolic tradition,' and she maintains that it is the duty of a Christian to receive the one and the other with equal veneration."

Some of the leading Protestant churches (Baptists are not Protestant in the commonly accepted use of the term) have accepted the Catholic position, and we shall see later in this study where that acceptance had led them.

Long before the Catholic Church came into existence, Paul warned against accepting the traditions of men: "Beware lest any man spoil you through philosophy and vain deceit after the tradition of men, after the rudiments of the world, and not after Christ. For in him dwelleth all the fulness of the Godhead bodily" (Col. 2:8,9).

Peter said: "You are not redeemed with corruptible things as silver and gold, from your vain conversation received by tradition from your fathers but by the precious blood of Christ as of a lamb without blemish and without spot." (See 1 Pet. 1:18,19.) So you see, we cannot go along with the Catholic position in the belief that it is the duty of the Christian to receive tradition and the Scripture with "equal veneration."

I must be a Baptist because of my acceptance of the Holy Scriptures as the inspired word of God, the infallible, unchanging, and unchangeable word of God.

## II. My Conception of God

I am a Baptist because my conception of God shapes my theology. For a definition of theology in the sense in which we use the term, we go to the dictionary: rational interpretation of religious faith, practice, and experience; the sum of beliefs held by an individual or group, regarding matters of religious faith or of ultimate concern. Theology is sometimes defined as a doctrine of biblical religion, a doctrinal declaration of the Scriptures systematically arranged. Paul had a theology but he did not always have it systematically arranged. This was true of others of the inspired writers.

Some sort of theology is an inescapable necessity. All religions, whether they be what we call pagan or Christian, have a theology. So we come to the question: What shapes my theology? We cannot minimize the importance of a proper answer to this question, since there is wrapped up in it my attitude toward the triune God; my attitude toward life here and hereafter; my attitude toward my fellowman here and toward the destiny of his soul after he leaves this world. What shapes my theology? The answer is: My conception of God shapes my theology. It is not only true of me as a Baptist but it is true of the Methodist, the Presbyterian, the Episcopalian, Church of Christ or Disciples, Pentecostal, Jehovah Witness, Christian Scientist, the Catholic, the agnostic, atheist, Hindu, and all the rest.

Let it be understood that we do not question the salvation of anyone because he is not of the Baptist faith! His conception of God may agree with mine: of God being the Father of the incarnate Son who lived a sinless life, died the substitutionary death on the cross, rose from the grave, ascended to heaven, sits at the right hand of God and is coming again someday. He may be one who believes in and has accepted the plan of salvation and has been born into the kingdom of God, but that is far from being all that is involved in one's theology. All that is involved is important, else the Holy Spirit would not have moved and inspired men to write it down as God's word to man.

### III. My Theology and the Church

My conception of God shapes my theology as to the church.

1. Jesus, the Founder and Head of the Church

"And I say also unto thee, That thou art Peter, and upon this rock I will build my church; and the gates of hell shall not prevail against it" (Matt. 16:18). (See also Eph. 5:23; Acts 2:38; Col. 1:18.)

To find the founder and head of a New Testament church, we must go back through the centuries: beyond Alexander Campbell, John Wesley, John Calvin, Martin Luther, Henry the VIII, and others, on back to him who said, "Upon this rock I will build my church."

Now with these and many others whom history records as founders or heads of the various religious bodies, and with their numerous beliefs and teachings which differ from the Scriptures as understood by Baptists, how am I to determine where I should take my stand? I cannot accept the theory that it makes no difference what one believes, just so he is sincere, or that one church is as good as another. I can think of no other realm in which we would take that position. Paul was sincere when he was persecuting the Christians. Multitudes of people are sincere in believing they are members of a New Testament church, whether it be Baptist or not. It may be because they have been taught by parents or others, or because they have not searched the Scriptures on the subject. So, my sincere desire to know what my church affiliation should be, leads me to search the Scriptures.

2. A Regenerate Church Membership

Baptists hold more consistently and tenaciously to this doctrine than does any other religious body. We believe that a visible church of Christ is a congregation of baptized believers. In New Testament days, only the redeemed were to be received as members of the church (Acts 2:47; 2:41). God's kingdom is a spiritual kingdom and only spiritually born people can be members of the church. Many people try to bypass the kingdom to get into the church. If one person who has never been born again has a scriptural right to have membership in a New Testament church, then no man need ever claim to have experienced the new birth before asking for membership in the church. Therefore, the church could not claim to be the body of Christ, since its members would not be in Christ, nor would Christ be in them.

3. The Ordinances of the Church

I am a Baptist because Baptists accept and follow the teachings of the Scriptures on the ordinances of the church.

(1.) Baptism

*The subject for baptism.*—A regenerate church membership leaves no place for infant baptism or baptismal regeneration. Infant baptism was established into law by the Catholic Church in A.D. 416. By this new law in fact, baptism became compulsory and thus vital New Testament doctrines were abrogated: believer's baptism and voluntary obedience in baptism.

Where did infant baptism and baptismal regeneration originate? Cardinal Gibbons, in his book *The Faith of Our Fathers,* said: "The church teaches that baptism is necessary for all, for infants as well as adults, and her doctrine rests on the following grounds: Our Lord said to Nicodemus: 'I say unto thee, unless a man be born again of water and the Holy Ghost, he cannot enter into the kingdom of heaven.' " Cardinal Gibbons goes on to say, "The Acts of the Apostles, although containing only fragmentary accounts of the ministry of the apostles, plainly *insinuate* that the apostles baptized children as well as grown persons. We are told for instance, that Lydia was baptized and her household, by St. Paul: and that the jailor was baptized and his family. The same apostle baptized also 'The household of Stephanas.' Although it is not expressly stated that there were children among these baptized families, the *presumption* is strongly in favor of the *supposition* that there were."

The Baptist position on believer's baptism as found in the New Testament is not based upon *insinuations, presumptions* or *suppositions,* but upon the word of God which no pope, group of cardinals, or church has a right to change.

*Mode of baptism.*—When and where did the practice of sprinkling or pouring originate? We quote again from *The Faith of Our Fathers* by Cardinal Gibbons. "The Baptists err in asserting that baptism by immersion is the only valid mode . . . as our Lord nowhere prescribes any special form of administering the sacrament, the church exercises her discretion in adopting the most convenient mode, according to the circumstances of time and place. For several centuries after the establishment of Christianity, baptism was usually conferred by immersion. . . . If immersion is the only valid form of baptism, what has become of the millions of souls who have been regenerated by the infusion or the aspersion of water in the Christian church?"

I would answer his question by saying that no soul, infant or adult, has ever been regenerated by infusion or aspersion of water. My conception of God is that he will not contradict himself by saying in one place, "for by grace are ye saved through faith; and that not of yourselves: it is the gift of God: not of works, lest any man should boast" (Eph. 2:8–9) and in another place declare that baptism is a means of salvation for either infant or adult. Cardinal Gibbon's conception of God is different to that of mine, since I cannot believe, that in view of the greatness of God and in view of what he has done for me, I have any right to sacrifice obedience for convenience. If God had taken the route of convenience, I think his Son would never have walked the road to Calvary. If one studies the Word of God and then believes that man can save himself, make himself worthy of being saved, or be saved at all apart from the shed blood of Christ and without a genuine personal confession and repentance of sin and a personal trust in and acceptance of Christ as Savior and Lord, his conception of the triune God must be different from mine.

(2.) The Lord's Supper

Baptists are probably more misunderstood by Protestants at this point than on any other phase of Bible doctrines. This is because Baptists, generally, do not invite members of churches of other faiths to observe the Lord's Supper with them. Many of them interpret it to mean that we do not believe they have been born again but, of course, this is not the case! Many think Baptists are selfish and narrow-minded at this point. The fact is, however, that most Protestant groups believe baptism should precede the Lord's table. So, it hinges to a very large degree, on the question: who has been scripturally baptized? The fact is, every reason that can be given for unity at the Lord's table, can be given for unity before we come to the Lord's table. Our Lord instituted the Supper. (See Matt. 26:26–30.)

The "broken bread" is symbolic of his flesh that is to be broken and the "fruit of the vine" is symbolic of his blood to be spilled. Else, why would he, in one sentence, use the word blood and in the next sentence, use the words, "the fruit of the vine"? The Supper, like baptism, has its own gospel message—a gospel in symbol. My conception of God will not let me change either of these, for to change the symbol is to destroy the gospel message which the Lord intended to be presented in them.

(3.) The Ordinances

The ordinances were given to the churches. The depository for them is divinely fixed. They were not deposited with individuals. What saith the Scriptures?

"Go ye therefore, and teach all nations, baptizing them in the name of the Father, and of the Son, and of the Holy Ghost" (Matt. 28:19). If Jesus was not speaking to his church, to whom was he speaking? (See also Mark 16:15.)

Paul must have thought the Lord's Supper was the responsibility of the church or he would not have gone into such detail in the eleventh chapter of his first letter to the church at Corinth. In verses 17 ff. he said, "Now in this that I declare unto you I praise you not, that you come together not for the better, but for the worse. For first of all, when you come together *in the church,* I hear that there be divisions among you; and I partly believe it. For there be also heresies among you. . . . When you come together therefore into one place, this is not to eat the Lord's Supper."

When Paul spoke of the church, he could not have meant churches of various denominations and faiths, for none of them were in existence for fifteen hundred years after Christ. If a church does not keep the ordinances in the manner and for the purpose for which they were given; if a church can discard or disregard any of the doctrines given to New Testament churches, tell me what they could handle loosely that is more sacred to the heart of our Lord than the ordinances of baptism and the Lord's Supper!

## IV. Conclusion

The half has not been told as to why I am a Baptist! Baptists believe in the lordship of Jesus Christ; a democratic form of church government for all Baptist churches. Baptists believe the believer is secure so long as the words everlasting and eternal mean everlasting and eternal and that God will never disown or disinherit one of his adopted children.

In this study I have not given much space to telling why I am not something other than a Baptist. As I understand it, if I tell why I am a Baptist, I will have answered most all questions as to why I am not something other than a Baptist.

Permit me to emphasize again that Baptists believe all who have been born into the kingdom of God by accepting and experiencing the plan of salvation which is clearly revealed in the holy Scriptures, will be in his kingdom forever. For those who have dared to change portions of the Word of God or who have accepted changes made by others, we leave them in the hands of a merciful God.

As for me, I must be Baptist because of my conception of God!

*A Denominational Executive*

## WHY I AM A BAPTIST
**Paul M. Stevens**

(Paul Stevens is a former pastor, and since 1951 director, Radio and Television Commission, Southern Baptist Convention, Fort Worth, Texas.)

### NOT BORN FREE—MADE FREE

When Jesus said, "If the Son therefore shall make you free, ye shall be free indeed," he threw down a challenge that has been picked up by millions in every succeeding generation.

But, his "freedom" is subject to only one definition. If there are those in any generation who cannot accept the deepest responsibilities of spiritual freedom, then they can no more serve him in spirit and in truth than can a blind man jump hurdles.

At heart, the great case for Christianity is a very real conflict of commitments. This is why it is such a great case. It is on a scale small enough to be personally experienced by all, but big enough to be symbolic to all. And there are those irreconcilable concepts of man's soul that are constantly at war. He is either totally and completely a free moral agent, or he wears fetters fashioned by some priesthood, secular or sacred, which may open or close heaven's doors to him on the basis of human whim.

At issue with me was the brightness of free election to worship as I pleased or accept the dark certitude that the "great case" versus my immortal soul was lost. Contending figures and terminologies strangely enough, eventually distilled themselves into two major decisions: Baptism first and then church membership.

Before I proceed I must reveal the fact that church membership had occurred for me as a child of ten. No spiritual experience is recallable by me to what, why, or by whose influence. Suffice to say, there seems to have been no conversion of heart, mind, or soul involved in this experience.

I grew up however, believing that a pair of eyes rested upon me, a shadow of divine interest passed over me in times of danger or personal distress. Like a cloud passing behind the woods in the winter, the feeling I was being watched was ever with me.

Sometimes you will wonder which is harder to bear: friendly indifference to the divine within you, or forthright hate toward anything or anyone who would threaten intervention in your affairs. And I felt threatened by this unseen presence.

In the sum of the experiences of life, one reaches benign acceptance. But, in youth, for me at least, my freedom was threatened and I felt resentment and fierce resistance.

The desire of my soul was to remain free. And any church affiliation or arrangement which I worked out with whatever God there was must grant me my freedom. That became the sticking point of my spiritual progress.

"Baptism and church membership next," they told me and that proved to be the major obstacle to me, in the shaping of my earliest longings to become an active effective Christian.

Soon after my conversion experience, I made purposeful visits to ministers of many faiths. Ignorance of detail, even an inability to know what questions to ask, caused me to almost stutter as I pressed each man, vicar, priest, pastor, or minister for answers to embryonic questions about what had happened to me, and what I should do. "Baptism and church membership next" seemed to sum up the answers I received.

Books of theology and church history were available to me but my thoughts did not turn in that direction.

I know I prayed, through ill-formed and half sentences and unspoken questions to God. "Who was I, where had I come from, what was I doing here, and where was I going?" Darkness stretched in all directions except one. I knew that something had happened to me which was leading every sense, appetite, and longing of my heart in another direction, completely different from anything I had ever hoped or dreamed of before.

A Bible had been packed in my few belongings by my parents when I set out on my own as a boy of fifteen or so. I soon found myself fingering its unfamiliar pages and staring uncomprehendingly at verses and chapters and books.

Then one day, I remember recalling the courageous statement of one Martin Luther, dredged up from history for me by some high-school teacher. "The just shall live by faith." Suddenly, it was as clear as a bell, a light thrown on a wilderness in which I found myself. "The just shall live by faith." That gave me a name for the experience I had received. I had found a "faith." In whom? Jesus Christ, of course!

But was it really that easy?

I began my Bible adventure in the book of Acts. The name appealed to me. "The Acts." Someone else had wanted to do something and their acts had been written down.

At first my eyes raced along the lines. I caught little or nothing until I came to what I later learned to call Acts 2:21: "And it shall come to pass, that whosoever shall call on the name of the Lord shall be saved."

So that is what had happened to me! I had been saved. From what? To what?

The pages of the book began to be irradiated with light, wrapped in brightness. I can't remember recalling the words "baptism and church membership next" for months. The ground forming under my feet had absolutely nothing to do with me or my actions. I was being saved and cleansed by the power of the Word of God. The desire to preach the gospel of the Son of God came upon me with such blinding force that all else in my life seemed to become unimportant and trivial.

I said, "seemed to become unimportant and trivial." There is a strange contradiction there, for actually everything in my life took on new meaning and new importance. But, the two experiences were running parallel to one another at this tide. They had not yet merged, as soon they would.

Some little cracks or crevices of our lives tend to pick up and hold bits and pieces of time and thought that cross over them from time to time. What schoolboy had not learned and shouted at play the word of Patrick Henry, "Give me liberty or give me death." Suddenly the resurrected phrase was being endlessly repeated in my mind. I counted trees on the campus to the tune, "Give me liberty or give me death."

I could not quiet the deathless phrase day or night. I was totally incapable of accounting for its repetitious power over my mind but there it was, nevertheless, through almost every waking moment. Then it came, slowly, ever so slowly.

My mother read to her little flock of six children many and many a night before we were sent to the cold white beds in the dark, dark bedrooms above. A story . . . a story about Patrick Henry. That is what was screaming at me to be remembered.

I found the volume in my library, fingered and read by my mother. I began to read it, as my mother had read. Here is the bit of history that struck in my mind.

Three Baptist ministers, Lewis and Joseph Craig, and an Aaron Bledsoe had been indicted in the colony of Virginia. They were before the court of law as the clerk read the charge against them. He was slowly reading a description of their crime: "For preaching the Gospel of the Son of God in the Colony of Virginia," when a plainly dressed man covered with dust from a long journey on horseback came striding into the courthouse and took his seat at the bar.

He was known to both the court and lawyers present, but a stranger to the crowd of spectators gathered for the occasion. He was Patrick Henry, arriving to volunteer his services in the ministers' defense.

He listened to the further reading of the indictment with marked attention, but it was the first sentence to fall on his ear upon his entrance into the room that set his mind aflame.

When time came for him to speak, he reached out his hand and took the paper from the clerk's hand and proceeded to address the court.

"May it please your worships: I think I heard read by the clerk as I entered this house the paper I now hold in my hand. If I understood rightly, the King's attorney has framed an indictment charging these three inoffensive persons with a crime of great magnitude, as disturbers of the peace. May it please the court, did I hear what I thought I heard? Did I hear it distinctly or was it a mistake of my own? Did I hear an expression, as if a crime, that these men, whom your worships are about to try for a misdemeanor are charged with . . . what?" The word reverberated between the naked wooden walls of the courtroom, "For preaching the gospel of the Son of God!"

Now he slowly began to pass among the crowd. In eloquent silence he moved from row to row among the spectators. And just as slowly he waved the indictment over his head in great circles. Then, lifting both hands and eyes to heaven, with peculiar and impressive energy, he exclaimed, "Great God!"

The exclamation, the outburst, the burst of feeling overpowered the entire audience.

Then he resumed:

"There are periods in the history of man, when corruption and depravity have so long debased the human character that man sinks under the weight of the oppressor's hand. He licks the hand that smites him and bows in passive obedience to the mandates of the despot. In this state of servility he receives his chains of perpetual bondage.

"But, may it please your worships, that day is past. From that period our fathers left the land of their nativity for settlement in these American wilds, for liberty! For liberty! To worship God according to their conceptions of Heaven's revealed will; from the moment they placed foot on American soil, and sought asylum in the deep forests of this land, from that moment despotism was crushed; her fetters of darkness were broken and Heaven's will was at least realized, man was free, free to worship God according to the Bible. Were it not for this, then all the sacrifices of the colonists have been in vain. In vain, I say, if we, their offspring, must still be oppressed and persecuted in this new world for what we believe.

"So, may it please your worships, let me ask again, for what are these men to be tried? This papers says, 'For preaching the Gospel of the Son of God! Great God,' he shouted again, 'for preaching the Gospel of the Savior to Adam's fallen race.' "

He paused, faced judge, then jury, then the crowded court. "What law have they violated," he cried, as he waved the indictment in large circles over his head, "What law have they violated?"

The prosecuting attorney turned pale while the judge and jury were ghastly expressions of alarm.

If only one moment, the judge recovered his senses and with authority said, "Sheriff, discharge these men."

From the moment of recall of the event, feeling my mother's deep indignation and triumph as she read it to us, I knew the die was cast. Men are saved by faith in the Son of God, no more no less, and no man is worthy of the name of follower of the Master unless his whole message is based on that one solid, eternal, believable, provable truth. Fortitude, battle, and final triumph mark the path of those who have believed it and lived it, and, among that noble throng marching down through history have been Baptists.

It was to be in Virginia that the first state constitutional provision for religious liberty was to be written by Thomas Jefferson and enacted into law. And, from it the first amendment of the Constitution of the United States was to trumpet to the world forever. "Man is free, free to worship God according to the Bible."

As a pastor, almost two-thirds of my sermonic material related to the New Testament came from the book of Acts, and I have never confronted a lost man or woman with the claims of Christ upon his or her life without quoting Acts 2:21: "And it shall come to pass, that whosoever shall call on the name of the Lord shall be saved."

I could not therefore say with truthfulness that I am a Baptist because of my study of systematic theology, though I have never found any obstacle to turn me aside while pursuing that course of study. I cannot say it was by birth or family heritage that led along the path of the Baptist faith. I certainly could not say that baptism first, and church membership next, had anything to do with it, as wise and important as those steps are when rightly defined and understood. It was a discovery, a scintillating, undimming discovery born in me by the Spirit of God that I was free, free to believe and follow one demanding, unchanging, unchallengeable fact of time and eternity, "Jesus is the Son of God, the Savior of the world and whosoever believeth in him hath eternal life."

The full liberty of my conscience had been found, freed, and forever committed. It is the foundation stone upon which my full knowledge and conviction has been stained, stamped, engraved, and inlaid forever. And every time my raised hand has trembled as though it would fall, it has been seized by a steadier hand and I am kept by him, suffering, triumphant, and sublime.

I am no religious iconoclast. I do not believe any man or grouping of men have a corner on the truth, to the exclusion of all other men. For the verse in Acts includes all as it beautifully expresses God's love for all men when it says, "And it shall come to pass that whosoever shall call upon the name of the Lord shall be saved." But, if words mean anything, then here is absolutism, though our day and age seeks to destroy the blacks and whites of any position. Here is ground for believing men to claim, and I am a Baptist because I found that Baptists believed it, all of it.

The ministry I perform today touches the lives of millions of people every week. Sometimes, most of the time, it is for only a fragile second or two that our ministry reaches the ears of their hearts. We cannot afford to deal in lengthly dissertations of theological profundity. We must speak simply, clearly, quickly, honestly, and effectively. We must say what the Savior said, in short, clear, understandable words. "If the son shall set you free, you shall be free indeed."

The nature of tragedy is to misunderstand or be misunderstood. Had I not come to know that bondage to Christ was absolute spiritual freedom, I should never have begun this grand adventure with my Lord.

At issue was not whether I should be free. It was whether the chains of selfishness were to be broken. The paradox was thus clearly revealed, "If the son shall make you free, then you are free indeed."

I refused to listen to the one who whispered in Eden, "Ye shall be as gods," and listened to the one who whispered, "Take up your cross and follow me."

*A Seminary President*

## WHY I AM A BAPTIST
**Grady C. Cothen**

(Dr. Grady C. Cothen is president of New Orleans Baptist Theological Seminary. Prior to going to that position he served as a pastor, as executive secretary of the Southern Baptist General Convention of California, and as president of Oklahoma Baptist University.)

When I was converted, I became a Baptist because my father was the pastor of the local Baptist church. Anything else would have been unthinkable. As a child S. Wilson, my Methodist friend across the street, challenged my Baptist positions on many of our doctrines. This began a series of experiences that caused me to examine carefully my own convictions. The positions stated in this paper have come into being after years of study, conversations, and investigations.

Baptists pride themselves on being a people of the Book. Generally it is believed that this sets us apart from others. In honesty, however, others also positionize themselves in the same manner. It is not enough simply to state a biblical basis for faith and then claim it as distinctive.

In fact, a Baptist position that is distinctive is a composite of many factors. It involves a view of the Bible as the inspired word of God but varying views of inspiration are possible. Perhaps the specifically Baptistic view of Scripture is that it is the sole rule of faith and practice. This eliminates statements of faith as creedal or binding. It provides room for several other aspects of doctrine that can be called Baptistic. We believe generally that our total faith is biblically based.

From this general beginning, we formulate positions on many aspects of our faith. For the lack of a better phrase, I am a Baptist because of our theology. It has a biblical orientation in most, if not all, of its phases. The sole rule of faith and practice stance gives a specific base for belief that is objective. This is to say that Scripture becomes the basis of theological decision. Opinions and judgments can be checked against this authority. Yet with the view of priesthood of believers, there is room for the specific leading of the Holy Spirit in the heart and experience of the believer. With such a view of Scripture—held by most Baptists—to the degree we try to write and enforce creedal statements, we compromise our Baptist distinctive.

Our theology thus derives its view of God from Scripture. The view of God in the main is easily understood. Perhaps the clearest and most moving portrait of the nature of God is to be found in John 3:16. The whole thrust of our Baptist theology centers in "For God so loved the world, that he gave his only begotten Son, that whosoever believeth in him shall not perish, but have everlasting life." This concept saturates the Scriptures. It views a loving but righteous God reaching out to sinful man, attempting to redeem the man at great cost to God himself. This love recognizes man for what he is and loves him in spite of it. God's purpose is to make the man his own child, cleanse, forgive, restore him, and give him a place in the family of God with eternal life. Such a theology presents God exactly as he ought to be in the light of the human problem. Any lesser view would not do, for it would not deal with reality.

The biblical view of God deals with man as he is. There is no overlooking the awful truth. There is no cheap dealing with sin. There is no avoidance of reality. There is an awesomely honest view of man, his sin, and his destiny. Equally there is a magnificent portrait of God surveying this carnage with his heart longing to rescue his bedeviled creature from himself. At the enormous cost of his Son, God is willing to enter into the arena with the consuming love necessary to right the situation. Upon his regeneration God takes the neophyte into himself to nurture and sustain him and make him a full partner in the task of world redemption. To the degree man responds to God, to that degree he is entrusted by the loving Father with responsibility commensurate with his abilities and dedication. The process of his personal development begins immediately and continues all his life.

The biblical emphasis on the dignity of the individual and the respect God has for him speaks to the needs of man in the modern world. This treatment sounds as though it might have been devised for this day by the most wise and benevolent of fathers, as indeed it was.

These elements of our theology are not exclusive to Baptists but are held by most. This theology is adequate for the situation that exists. It is impossible for me to imagine another that is. Indeed to meet our needs God must be as he is and the record of his character and nature must be available for our guidance as it is in the Scriptures. This theology meets the intellectual requirements created in us. It meets the needs of man as he is without the compromise of God as he is. It holds out to man the highest possible ideals for his maturing. The impossible challenge is there, yet allows for remarkable development of the individual.

Baptists generally insist on a biblically oriented ethical system. The nature of man's relationship with God requires that man's ethical system seek the highest possible good for every man. Nowhere is such an idea more positively and succinctly stated than in the Scripture, "Thou shalt love thy neighbor as thyself." Here is an impossible but challenging commandment. This is instruction that recognizes the dignity and worth of the individual but not at the expense of others.

This law provides for the sharpest possible self-imposed limitation on conduct. It is inherently designed for personal development. It is a goad to the careless, a challenge to the conscientious, and a guide to the sincere. Its observance guarantees justice to others. Its high idealism represents a constant check on and stimulus to morally and ethically acceptable behavior.

The ethical ideal is explicated in its endless involvements throughout the Scriptures. The Beatitudes give voice to some of its implications. The First Epistle of John discusses its relationships. James insists that a son of God be a doer of these things and not a hearer only. It is perhaps most movingly and beautifully discussed in 1 Corinthians 13.

This ethical standard motivated by the active Holy Spirit in each life provides endless spiritual exercise. It is an unattainable ideal requiring constant effort. The example of Christ is always before the believer. The power of God is available for the earnest soul's assistance. Each is in eternal debt to the rest of us. One of the highest expressions of the ideal of love is work of the believer to bring others into the saving relationship with Christ.

The rights and responsibilities of the individual involved in the ethical standards of the Scripture relate directly to the polity principles of Baptists. The ethical ideal is not possible as a principle controlling life apart from the guarantees of the priesthood of each believer and the resultant polity. These elements are so interrelated and interdependent that one leads logically to the other. They cannot be separated if a true Baptist position is to be maintained.

It is at this point of combination of these two emphases based on the theology of the love of God that Baptists achieve a true distinctive.

In this stage of human history certain needs emerge as being particularly important. The young people have emphasized these especially in the last few years. With the growing depersonalization of a highly technologized society, the problems of personhood emerged in an unusual way. The issues of the dignity of the individual and the worth of every person are particularly pertinent to the modern social scene. Freedom of thought is especially important in a time of consolidation of power structures at every level of life. The individual's freedom of decision and thought has tribute paid to it at every level of life. Mighty forces militate against it, however, as a pluralistic society becomes more and more complex and necessity demands increasing regimentation in many areas of life. These are everywhere evident in education, in social structures, in economic life and increasingly in religion.

These are illustrated by the struggle within the Catholic Church to achieve an increasing share of freedom from ecclesiastical control. Nowhere is the idea better illustrated than in the struggle of the Catholic clergy against the rule of celibacy enforced by the hierarchy. The polity of other bodies that use various patterns of ecclesiastical authority is under constant pressure.

Baptists begin in the structure of polity with the fundamental unit of the individual—a priest before God. Every individual is a priest. The involvements of this seemingly simple doctrine are endless and often poorly understood. Of course, it means that each individual has the right of direct access to God. From a human view, he is able to represent himself and his interests directly to his Creator with no need for another to mediate or prompt or provide rules or control. It means further that he is responsible for himself in relationships to God. This is both a burden and a blessing. He is free of strictures so that he may act independently, but he must accept the responsibility for his acts. This gives him a responsible role in God's plan of things. Not only does he become liable for his actions, but he becomes responsible for the Kingdom enterprise. The sons of God relate directly to the Father and receive instructions and discipline from him.

Ecclesiastical control over an individual is nonexistent. The church as the next logical step is also independent and autonomous. Its prime responsibility is to its Lord. The corporate body of Christians responding as individuals to the leading of the Lord theoretically can act in concert in the affairs of the church. More often than not they accomplish this miracle. At any point the individual dissents as a matter of conscience, he is free to say so or even disassociate himself from the congregation without ecclesiastical penalty. The democracy of the local congregation is a well-known fact. A less often articulated fact is that this democracy is exercised biblically under the authority of Christ himself.

Our polity considerations produce a remarkably free ministry which has wide latitude to respond to God's leading in the affairs of the church. When both the minister and the church respond to the theology, ethical, and polity demands of the Scriptures under the tutelage of the risen Lord, harmony prevails and the church prospers. The freedom of the minister may be limited by the will of the congregation but again he and they are free to sever the connection and pursue the dictates of their consciences.

In logical progression beginning with the free individual under God, a church is created by a gathering of these individuals. The church in fulfilling its functions is a free and independent unit also under the direction of God. No ecclesiastical authority controls it. Its membership has the final word on its membership and activities. As the church looks beyond its community, it recognizes certain tasks that require the cooperation of other churches, for example, higher education.

As a result churches form associations with other churches to establish cooperative effort to carry out their corporate purposes. The association is composed of representatives from the churches and abides by the decisions of those gathered. It is independent and controls its own membership and purposes. A church does not have authority over it and is not subject in turn to it. On a district or state level, conventions are formed of representatives of the churches—not the associations—and is independent and autonomous. A church does not control it nor is subject to it. In the same manner the national convention is independent and autonomous—subject to its membership gathered from the churches on a given occasion and time. It may delegate certain responsibilities to boards and create agencies to carry out those functions, but each is finally responsible through the board to the convention.

The lines of ecclesiastical authority are thus difficult for many to understand. Theoretically, where no authority exists over individuals, ministers, and churches, no unified program would be possible practically. Continuity would be difficult if not impossible since each phase of work would be subject to the mood or desire of the assembled body of control. In point of reality however, there is a remarkable continuity of work and a very high degree of stability in the agencies and institutions created by these independent and autonomous bodies at every level.

The principle and person of cohesion is the Holy Spirit. A multitude of people responding to the lordship of Christ find themselves bound together by common concerns and dedicated to the same general purposes. Missions, evangelism, education, and other causes become the rallying point for individuals, churches, associations, and conventions.

We are not bound together by mechanical external bonds or ecclesiastical or denominational control. Each person and unit are more or less bound by their bondage to Christ. As each responds to Christ, he finds himself related to others whom he loves who are equally bound to Christ. This achieves a degree of harmony of purpose impossible to achieve by organization or structure or authority.

Practical men with considerable astuteness in organization believe that this kind of organization cannot exist long. Especially it cannot be constituted of people of widely diverse background, status, interests, and varying degrees of sophistication.

But it works! The cohesion is in the nature of the sons of God and in the work of the Holy Spirit. He binds us to the purposes of God and thus to each other. Our human variations result in enough difference in forms, methods, and techniques to meet the needs of many different people. He gives similarity enough to make the organizations function.

Other religious groups hold to one or more of these outlined beliefs. In combination, however, under the leading and power of God, they have made possible a strong virile denomination that has endured the gales of theological controversy, organizational problems, and some lean years. This kind of denomination has built into its nature and structure the finest sort of self-limitations. It is capable of self-criticism and renewal. At any point that God's people are willing to follow his leading, reform, change, and progress are possible. Whenever God can capture the minds of even a substantial minority in a church or convention with our polity, change in his will can occur. Ecclesiastical authority is in fact in the hands of the people as it ought to be. If the people are in the hand of God, his purposes can prosper.

For all these reasons and many more that space prohibits mentioning, I am a Baptist.

*A Layman*

## WHY I AM A BAPTIST
**Owen Cooper**

(Owen Cooper is a Mississippi business executive. He is very active as deacon and leader in his church, First Baptist, Yazoo City, Mississippi, and in the denomination. He is a vice-president of the Baptist World Alliance, chairman of the Southern Baptist Convention Executive Committee, and a former president of the Mississippi Baptist Convention.)

I was born on a hill farm (not in a hospital) eight miles northeast of Vicksburg, Mississippi. I grew up in a Christian home (father, Baptist; mother, Presbyterian) enjoying the virtues of the early nineteen hundred's rural living and accepting, without protest, but with challenge, the problems of life in the hill section of Mississippi. Among my earliest childhood memories was attending Bethlehem Church, traveling in a horse- or mule-drawn vehicle, and participating in "Children's Day." We lived in a sparsely settled area. Because of the remoteness of the church or perhaps for other reasons I do not know, we were not regular in attendance.

Immediately after World War I my father went into the dairy business and together with his three sons assumed the task of milking an increasing number of dairy cows twice a day. This tied the family close to home because of a 6:00 A.M. and a 5:00 P.M. daily responsibility.

During my high school years a Presbyterian evangelist (E. J. Bulgin) came to Vicksburg for a revival meeting in a twenty-five hundred seat temporary tabernacle, with a sawdust floor, erected for the exclusive purpose of the meeting.

It was during this meeting that I acknowledged my sins, accepted Christ as my Savior, publicly professed him as my Lord, and asked God's Spirit to dwell within; guiding, counseling, motivating and giving insight. *This is a Baptist practice.*

It has always been of interest to me that I was led to the Lord by a Presbyterian minister, for, after all, it is by the grace of God, through faith in Jesus and the work of the Holy Spirit that we become children of the Almighty. It is not the result of the belief of the preacher. *This is a Baptist belief.*

The work of a "witnesses" in the miracle of salvation is one of communication. Transformation is the result of the work of the Holy Spirit. The important thing is "what is communicated" and not who is the communicator. As Christians we all have a responsibility to be communicators or witnesses. *This is a Baptist belief.*

Although my family occasionally attended the First Baptist Church or the First Presbyterian Church in Vicksburg, Mississippi, the daily, demanding duties of the dairy did not make it practical to consider baptism or church membership immediately following my conversion.

Upon graduation from high school I attended Mississippi State University. For the first seven months of the school year I regularly attended the church of my mother's choice. I could have no greater ambition than to be the type of Christian represented by my mother.

During this period of time I was reading my Bible, reading other books, and engaging in prayerful soul searching; seeking a church and denominational relationship which I felt would be most meaningful to me. This period of soul searching resulted in my being baptized, by immersion, at the First Baptist Church, Starkville, Mississippi, in April of 1926. Upon retrospect I do not regret delaying baptism. To me baptism is not a *means of salvation;* it is an *act of obedience* to be voluntarily entered into by an accountable individual. It's efficacy lies in the inevitable spiritual uplift that comes when anyone feels he is obeying God and publicly demonstrates becoming a part of the body of Christ, the church. *This is an accepted Baptist belief.*

During college days I was quite active in the local church, in the Baptist Student Union, and in YMCA work. I felt God was calling me in some manner for some service. I sought specific instructions from his call. One year after graduation I went to Leland, Mississippi, to teach school, taking three books important to me at that time: first a Bible; second, a catalog of the Law School of the University of Mississippi; and third, a catalog of the Southern Baptist Theological Seminary. This was in 1930, at the beginning of the great depression. I taught school in Leland five years and during this time I was not led to law school at Ole Miss or to the Seminary.

I have a growing conviction God's call is not restricted to the ministry or the field of Christian education or to the field of church music. God has a plan or purpose for every life. He has a "call" for each person who will surrender, and listen, and yield, and commit. There was a feeling that I, too, was a "priest," because every believer is a priest. And as such, I accepted the "office" of a priest, as revealed in God's word, and I also attempted to accept the "servanthood" of my "priesthood" by becoming what, for want of a better term, may be expressed as a "lay minister." Believing that all Christians are servants (ministers) and, as servants, all Christians should perform the role of a Christian servant, I found satisfaction in my denominational relationship for *this, too, is a Baptist belief.*

I have always been somewhat of an "activist." I have enjoyed and appreciated the freedom offered in the Baptist church and the Baptist denomination to work within the structure for continuation, for change, for improvement, or for innovation. I have never felt inhibited because of my age, lack of status, or that my "cause" was not popular. My interest in youth, BSU work, lay involvement, home mission outreach, foreign mission expansion, increasing financial support of the total church program, and Christian education has led me to be involved in many proposals and to have worked on many committees in connection with Baptist affairs.

Although I may have engaged in many church and nonchurch related "good works" I believe that an accountable person is saved by faith and not by work. *This is a Baptist belief.*

The democratic structure of the business meeting in the local church, associational meeting, meeting of the state convention, and the meeting of the Southern Baptist Convention has always provided a forum for the expression of ideas and a means by which proposals could be made in connection with any valid and worthy interest. Because of this democratic process that permits each individual to become involved to the extent of his desire, I have found great satisfaction in my relationships as a Baptist.

Through the years I have enjoyed reading, studying, and attempting to teach the Bible. I believe the Bible to be God's holy, inspired and sufficient word. I believe the truth of the Bible will speak to anyone who reads it with an open mind, with a searching soul, and a hungry heart. I believe that each such person can be led by the Holy Spirit to appropriate the truth of the Scripture to his own life in a peculiar and unique way to make the Scripture more meaningful to him than can possibly be so when the only interpretation is made by and accepted from another. This does not mean that others, especially worthy scholars, cannot make remarkable contributions in my understanding the Scripture. It does mean though, that when I expose myself to the Scripture and the Scripture speaks to me that it becomes personal in my life and meaningful in my Christian experience. This is consistent with the Baptist position that each normal person is competent to read, understand, and interpret the Scripture, under guidance of the Holy Spirit, as the rule and conduct of his own life.

As a Baptist layman, reared under modest circumstances and introduced to the working world at the beginning of the great depression, "things" assumed a disproportionate position in my life. Security was too often equated in terms of the assurance of a job, a favorable bank balance and a growing investment portfolio. To counterbalance the appeal of the secular, I needed a continuing religious experience that magnified the spiritual, that taught it was more blessed to give than to receive, that faithfully and without apology emphasized sharing (beginning with the tithe), and that continually reminded me, despite my inherent skepticism, that treasures in heaven were most important and that a man should not exchange his soul for the "world."

This I found to be a rule of faith and practice in each of the five Baptist churches in which I have held membership. In their own peculiar way, each of these churches has helped me in the ever increasing tug-of-war between God and mammon, and I have needed all that my Baptist church afforded to tip the struggle slightly toward God's side.

Man, without faith in God, is lost and this I believe. Thus, as a Christian, I carry a burden to go to *all the world* and preach and teach and make disciples. As a "witness" I have not been able to escape the feeling of this burden, but how can a lone individual, even with a burden of concern, become meaningfully involved in a great program of local, national, and worldwide witness. In the Baptist church I have found a channel through which this desire can be directed and by so doing a part of the burden to tell others has been lifted.

My local Baptist church has always had programs of visitation, Bible study directed toward commitments to Christ, projects of personal soul-winning, revival meetings, crusades, and other methods useful in confronting lost persons with the claims of Christ.

Through cooperative mission activities I have had a part in an ever growing witness throughout the nation. Training programs for laymen, evangelism conferences for pastors, crusades, and campaigns have been combined with the limited, but effective, use of radio, television, city missions, pioneer missions, language missions, Scripture and tract distribution, and distribution of other published materials to call men to Christ.

The world is the mission field of the Christian. Through my church, associated with others, there has been developed a great world mission thrust with upward of twenty-five hundred missionaries serving in seventy-six countries, with the principal objective being to tell the "good news" and to confront all men, of all countries, of all races and cultures, with the truth of God.

Through salvation man's life can be changed; changed lives can change homes, communities, nations and the world—this my church teaches. I want to have a meaningful part in this great miracle of change.

This is the objective of the Baptist church—this is my objective—this is why I am a Baptist.

# SECTION III

## Baptist Distinctives

## An Analysis of Basic Baptist Beliefs
Joe T. Odle

## BAPTIST DISTINCTIVES

There are approximately thirty-one million Baptists in the world today. How could anyone say why all of them are Baptists or what makes them what they are? It is an impossible task to speak for every Baptist, but one can find the common denominator of Baptist distinctives, the beliefs which characterize most of them. While these will not fit every individual Baptist, they will depict rather clearly what makes people Baptists, and what differentiates them from other groups. In the following pages we discuss the principles which we have found to be the distinctives which set Baptists apart from others.

In coming to our conclusions concerning these, we examined carefully each of the statements which are included in the earlier part of this book, both the shorter testimonies and the sermons. Then we turned to more than fifty other books by Baptist authors which dealt with Baptists, their doctrines and their history. Out of these came the emphases which we consider to be Baptist distinctives, according to what Baptists say about themselves and their doctrines. We have concluded that these are the things which make Baptists what they are, and which attract men to the Baptist position.

In making this study we have found one principle which appears to be a part of almost every testimony on "Why I Am a Baptist," whether it be those in this book or those appearing elsewhere. Almost every person who writes or speaks on his reasons for his faith, attributes to some person the responsibility, at least in part, for his being what he is. Usually this is in the home and family, but sometimes it is a pastor, an evangelist, a Sunday School teacher, or a neighbor or friend. One of the reasons men give for being Baptist is that influence that one or more persons has had upon them. This, however, hardly can be called a distinctive, since it also would be true of most people of other groups.

Neither is it the common name "Baptist" which marks these people as a distinctive group. This does not mean that they do not wear the name Baptist proudly, for they do. After all, it is a New Testament name which they bear. The name Baptist appears fifteen times in the New Testament. Evidently, John was called "the Baptist" before he baptized. The Bible speaks of him, the first New Testament preacher, as a Baptist. It is a good name. Dr. Charles Koller, long-time president of Northern Baptist Theological Seminary in Chicago, asked, "If John was not the first Baptist, who was?" Furthermore, the Lord Jesus Christ took some of these men who had been baptized by this first Baptist preacher, and used them as the nucleus of his church. Yet, it is not their name which sets Baptists apart as a distinct people. It is their beliefs.

What are the basic Baptist beliefs? Some declare there is no such thing as a Baptist position since Baptists are not a creedal people, and do not require of their members that they accept certain doctrinal positions. Yet, something does make men Baptists, and does distinguish them from members of other denominations. They are not Methodists, Presbyterians, Episcopalians, Roman Catholics or members of one of the more than two hundred other denominations now in existence. Why? There is only one reason, and that is that their doctrines are different. They are separated from others by what they believe.

As we study the history of Baptists, analyze statements of faith adopted by the various Baptist groups, and consider the Baptist position as it is enunciated in books and other writings, we make an amazing discovery. *There is no single distinctive doctrine which makes men Baptists. It is their position on a number of beliefs, which when taken together, make them a distinctive people.*

Almost every doctrine which Baptists profess, also is held by some other Christian group. It is only when a number of the doctrines and beliefs are put together that the Baptist position begins to emerge, and their distinctiveness as a denomination is seen.

Baptists hold many of the great doctrines of the Christian faith in common with many other Christian groups, especially the evangelical groups. With them, they believe in God the Father, the Son, and the Holy Spirit; in the creation and fall of man, and in the curse of sin upon the human race; in God's purposes in provision of redemption for man; in the incarnation of Jesus Christ; in his death, burial, and resurrection; in his ascension to heaven, and in his promised return; in the church; in death and judgment; in heaven and hell; and in the many other fundamental basic truths of the Christian faith. In many of these the Baptist position differs very little from that of others, but in certain ones there is a distinctive interpretation, and it is that which makes men Baptists. These we must see and understand if we are to comprehend why Baptists are Baptists and not something else.

What are these distinctives? Before beginning to discuss those which our research has led us to believe them to be, let us see what other men have said they are.

Baptist distinctives have been summarized by many men. Space forbids that we use more than a few of them here. Consider the following from respected and honored Baptist leaders and theologians:

1. Dr. J. E. Dillard, long-time Southern Baptist pastor and leader in this century, listed Baptist distinctives as follows: (1) Christ is Lord. (2) The New Testament is the only rule of faith and practice. (3) The soul is competent in religion. (4) A regenerated church membership. (5) The church is a spiritual democracy. (6) The ordinances are symbolic of historic facts, both experimental and historical.

2. Dr. B. H. Carroll, pastor and teacher in Texas, one of the fathers of Southwestern Baptist Theological Seminary, and prolific author, named Baptist distinctives as follows: (1) The New Testament is the law of Christianity. (2) Individual responsibility to

God. This means no proxies, no infant baptism, and no priests. (3) Salvation is essential to baptism and church membership. (4) The church is a spiritual body; separated from the state; a particular congregation and not an organized denomination; a pure democracy; the supreme court in Christ's kingdom; the ordinances are symbols of great spiritual truths. (5) God has an order in the gospel of his Son.

3. Dr. Edward T. Hiscox, Baptist writer of an earlier day, lists Baptist distinctives as follows: (1) Baptism by immersion. (2) Baptism only of those who have exercised a saving faith in Christ and are regenerated by the Spirit. (3) Church membership only for those who have been regenerated, and have been scripturally baptized. (4) Communion should be taken by members of the church alone, being such persons as are regenerated and baptized on a profession of faith in Christ. (5) Churches are independent and governed by their own members. (6) Scriptural officers should be pastors and deacons.

4. Dr. George W. McDaniel, distinguished Southern Baptist pastor and author listed the following "doctrines which are distinctive with us": (1) The New Testament is the sole and sufficient rule of faith and practice. (2) Individual responsibility to God for performance and duty. (3) A church is a body of baptized believers, equal in rank and privilege, administering its own affairs under the headship of Christ.

5. Dr. E. Y. Mullins, long-time president of Southern Baptist Theological Seminary and distinguished Baptist theologian and leader, uniquely presented Baptist principles as six axioms of religion:

"Now, the relation of Baptists to this great theological movement has not been adequately recognized and needs defining afresh. Behind our contentions as to baptism and communion and related topics lie a group of great and elemental principles. These principles are religious ultimates, nay they are axioms, which the instructed religious consciousness of man cannot repudiate. I sum them and submit them as a statement of the basis at once for a new Baptist apologetic and a platform for universal adoption.

"(1) The theological axiom: *The holy and loving God has a right to be sovereign.* Time forbids that I elaborate this statement in its implications as to the incarnation, and as to Christianity as a religion of the Divine initiative.

"(2) The religious axiom: *All men have an equal right to direct access to God.* This principle is fatal to the practice of infant baptism and to the idea of a human priesthood.

"(3) The ecclesiastical axiom: *All believers have equal privileges in the church.* Hierarchies and centralized authorities disappear under the operation of this principle.

"(4) The moral axiom: *To be responsible man must be free.* This is an elemental truth which cannot receive thoroughgoing application where ecclesiastical bonds of mere authority are absent.

"(5) The social axiom: *Love your neighbor as yourself.* That makes the kingdom of God the goal of the social movement.

"(6) The religio-civic axiom: *A free church in a free state.* For this principle Baptists have ever stood. Without it the future of theology and of the church is fraught with extreme peril."

6. Sydnor L. Stealey, theologian and president of Southeastern Baptist Theological Seminary, taught the distinctives as follows: (1) The holy Scriptures are the final source of authority regarding all matters of faith and practice. (2) A regenerated church membership. (3) Baptism by immersion of believers only. (4) Two ordinances with a symbolic meaning: baptism and the Lord's Supper, in that order. (5) The priesthood of the believer—individual access to God. (6) The congregational government of the church. (7) The complete separation of church and state. (Presented as remembered by a former student. He stated that Dr. Stealey required his students to memorize these Baptist distinctives.)

7. Dr. John A. Broadus, distinguished Baptist theologian and one of the founders of Southern Baptist Theological Seminary, lists the distinctives as: (1) The Bible alone is a religious authority; and

in regard to Christian institutions the direct authority is of course the New Testament. (2) The church ought to consist only of persons making a credible profession of faith, of faith in Christ. (3) Officers, government, and ceremonies in the church ought to be such only as the New Testament directs. (4) Churches are to be independent.

8. George W. Truett, Southern Baptist pastor and world Baptist leader said, (1) The absolute lordship of Christ. (2) The Bible our rule of faith and practice. (3) Direct individual approach to God. The Baptist message is nonsacerdotal, non-Sacramentarian, and nonecclesiastical. (4) The ordinances are symbols. (5) The church is a pure democracy. (6) Religious liberty.

On the basis of these statements, and the many other discussions which I have found, and out of the experience of my own ministry as a Baptist preacher, I have chosen the subjects discussed in the following brief chapters, as the distinctive principles which I have found men say make them Baptists. Perhaps every principle has not been included, and I may have omitted some particular truth which affected some individual, but considering Baptists as a group, I am convinced that these listed principles are the basic distinctives of their faith.

Of course, they should be recognized for what they are, the conclusions of one Baptist writer and student. Some other student of our faith might compile a different list. One Baptist never can say positively what all other Baptists believe. Nevertheless, every effort has been make to look objectively at Baptists and to see what makes them what they are.

## THE BIBLE

Perhaps there is no doctrinal position which does more to unify Baptists as a distinctive people, than their beliefs about the Bible.

1. The Baptist position may best be expressed by quoting the article on the Scriptures, found in the Statement of Faith adopted

by Southern Baptists in 1963.

The Statement of Faith says, "The Holy Bible was written by men divinely inspired and is the record of God's revelation of himself to man. It is a perfect treasure of divine instruction. It has God for its author, salvation for its end, and truth, without any measure of error, for its matter. It reveals the principles by which God judges us; and therefore is, and will remain to the end of the world, the true center of Christian union, and the supreme standard by which all human conduct, creeds and religious opinions should be tried."

It is not even necessary to discuss this statement since it is very clear. It is not a creedal statement, and therefore is not binding upon any Baptist, yet it is an enunciation of what Baptists believe about the Bible. It presents the authorship and the authority of the Word of God.

2. While Baptist believe that the whole Bible is the word of God, and they accept it all, they recognize that the church is a New Testament institution, and that the organization, teachings, and programs for the church are found in the New Testament. Dr. B. H. Carroll summarized the Baptist position well when he said, "The New Testament is the law of Christianity. All the New Testament is the Law of Christianity. The New Testament is all the law of Christianity. The New Testament will always be the Law of Christianity." It is on the basis of this that Baptists can claim that the New Testament is their creed; that every doctrine which they teach is from the New Testament, and that every doctrine of the New Testament is Baptist doctrine.

This acceptance of the Scriptures separates Baptists from other groups, who may claim to hold the same position but actually change it. It separates from those who take away from the New Testament, failing to carry out some of its clear commands; it separates from those who add to the New Testament, accepting as of equal value the statements of councils of men and of men themselves; it separates from those who change the New Testament, substituting something else for its teachings. To the Baptists the New Testament, and the New Testament alone, must be the one and the final authority for all that they do and preach.

Baptists believe the Bible, preach the Bible, and make the Bible the very center of their teaching and training program. To them the whole Christian faith is based upon the Bible, and especially upon the New Testament and nothing can take its place.

Dr. E. Y. Mullins said, "For Baptists there is one authoritative source of religious truth and knowledge. To that source they look in all matters relating to doctrine, to polity, to the ordinances, to worship and Christian living. That source is the Bible."

Dr. Mullins also said, "Behind this sufficiency and authoritativeness of the Scriptures of the Old and New Testaments is their inspiration. Holy men of God spoke as they were moved by the Holy Spirit. There are many ways of explaining the method of inspiration which men have adopted. We cannot discuss them here. The fact is the supreme thing. The Bible is God's message to man given to supply the needs of his religious life. When we find that message, we have God's truth to us which is all that we need for religious knowledge, faith, and obedience."

We could quote page after page from other men who make clear the Baptist position on the Bible as the Word of God. It is not needful. Sufficient to say, Baptists do believe the Bible and accept the authority of the Bible.

3. There is an amazing relationship between the Bible and Baptists. The Bible has a tendency to turn men toward the Baptist position. Baptist doctrines are the doctrines of the New Testament. Baptists have not added to or taken away from the meaning of the Word. The result is that when men study the Bible alone, they find themselves seeing truths which Baptists teach. Actually if a person follows the New Testament and that alone, it likely will lead him into the Baptist faith. It has happened many times.

A notable example is found in the *Memoir of James P. Boyce,* by John A. Broadus. "The late Dr. Oncken assured the writer that in forming a new church at Hamburg (Germany), A.D. 1834, the constituent members first resolved that they would shut themselves up entirely to the apostolic model as found in the New Testament. They therefore devoted themselves for some time to prayer and the exclusive study of that book as an inspired Church Manual; and on comparing their results, to their surprise they found themselves compelled to form a church in accord with the Baptist churches in England and America. There is nothing strange in this; the New Testament is ever the same, and it is but natural that when the devout mind is left free from all standards but this, with a determination to follow it in the most simple-hearted manner, it should produce the same stamp of New Testament churches everywhere and always."

Thus we can say the Bible is the book for Baptists.

We feel that the Bible makes us Baptists.

## THE LORDSHIP OF JESUS CHRIST

Many Baptists say that one of their distinctives is the lordship of Christ. They are not alone in this belief, but certainly it is one of the essential keys to the Baptist position.

Baptists believe the Bible is the Word of God, and in the Bible they find the Lord Jesus Christ. He is central in all that they are and do.

The Lord Jesus Christ!

One with the Father through all the eternities, even before the world was.

"All things were made by him; and without him was not anything made that was made" (John 1:3).

Yet he laid aside the robes of his glory, and took upon him the form of a man.

He was conceived by the Holy Spirit, and born of a virgin.

He took upon himself human flesh, so that he was deity in human form. He was very God and very man.

Even in the flesh, Paul tells us, "For in him dwelleth all the fulness of the Godhead bodily" (Col. 2:9). Dr. Herschel H. Hobbs says this is the greatest verse in the Bible.

He was God, and he was man. He walked among men, revealing God to men.

His purpose in coming was clear. He "appeared to put away sin by the sacrifice of himself" (Heb. 9:26), so that sinful men could be saved. He came to purchase redemption for us, so that God could "be just, and the justifier of him which believeth" (Rom. 3:26).

He purchased our redemption with his own blood, and "the blood of Jesus Christ his Son cleanseth us from all sin" (1 John 1:7).

Nothing else can save men . . . nothing they can do . . . nothing other men can do for them. To Baptists, "There is none other name under heaven given among men, whereby we must be saved" (Acts 4:12).

Christ died for our sins.

He was buried.

He rose from the dead on the third day.

The grave was empty. The Father raised him from the dead in bodily resurrection. He was alive forever more.

He returned to heaven, to prepare a place for his own, and to ever make intercession for them.

He is coming again. He said he would. The world's one hope, the world's greatest coming event, is the second coming of our Lord.

Then he will bring to consummation all of the purposes of God for man . . . his dealings with the world system . . . the judgment of men . . . the new heaven and the new earth . . . and hell. All of it under his power, and all things will be completed in him at his return.

Yet he lives on the earth today, in the hearts of believers, through the Holy Spirit. He is their life, their strength, their leader, their head. He truly is the Lord of all.

This is the Baptist message, this is the Baptist faith, this is the center of all that Baptists are and do.

## SALVATION

If there is one main issue that divides Baptists from others, more than anything else, it is, "How are men saved?" In his book, *The Church and the Ordinances,* Buell H. Kazee says: "Our divisions (with other denominations) are not limited to the nonessentials; we are divided on the main issue—how we are saved."

If there is any one matter which concerns Baptists, it is the salvation of their fellowmen. Their belief about man's need for salvation, and God's provision of it, makes this an imperative issue. Others may consider personal salvation a secondary matter, as they pursue their efforts to redeem society by social action, but to the Baptist nothing is so important as getting men saved. There are several reasons for this Baptist conviction.

1. Baptists believe that every man is a sinner, and that every person in the world needs to be saved. They believe the Bible when it says "in Adam all die" (1 Cor. 15:22) and "All have sinned, and come short of the glory of God" (Rom. 3:23). The Bible clearly reveals that man is a sinner both in his nature and in his practice, and Baptists believe that. They reject the theories and philosophies of men which state that man is innately good. They know that this is not so, both because God has revealed the true nature of man in his Word, and also because the evidence of sin in men's lives is seen everywhere. In his sinful state man is unfit for fellowship with God, and is under the curse that rests upon sin. In order to be acceptable to God, man's nature must be changed, and his life pattern must be altered. He must be born again. He must have a re-creation, making him a new creature in Christ. Man, by himself, however, is unable to change his nature, or to do that which would make him acceptable to God. All the education, culture, good

works, and other achievements of man cannot change his condition or make him a new creature. Baptists see man, even at his best, as hopeless and helpless within himself, as far as reaching God is concerned. What, then can man do? Nothing! God has done it!

2. God in his love for man, and in his mercy upon man, has provided a way of salvation. Man could not save himself, so God has provided salvation for him. That salvation of God is in his Son, the Lord Jesus Christ. On the cross Christ died for our sins and made atonement for sin. Paul said in 2 Corinthians 5:21: "For he hath made him to be sin for us, who knew no sin; that we might be made the righteousness of God in him." Baptists believe the prophet Isaiah when he says, "He was wounded for our transgressions, he was bruised for our iniquities: the chastisement of our peace was upon him; and with his stripes we are healed. All we like sheep have gone astray; we have turned every one to his own way; and the Lord hath laid upon him the iniquity of us all" (Isa. 53:5–6). Christ not only died for our sins but he rose again, conquered death, and lives forever, and one day will return to earth to consummate God's purpose in redemption.

3. Baptists believe in the priesthood of the believer. This means that man is responsible to God for himself and that he can and must approach God for himself. There is no hierarchy, no priest, and no human mediator between God and man. This excludes infant baptism, priestly intermediaries, and substitutes for personal faith. Man can come to God for himself! Man must come to God for himself!

4. This salvation which God has provided in giving his Son, and which Christ has purchased for us with his own blood, is offered to man by grace alone. Grace is God's unmerited favor. It is God's love, offering to sinful man a redemption that he neither deserves nor can merit. It is God's free gift, and all that man can do is accept it by repenting of his sin and believing upon the Lord Jesus Christ.

Salvation cannot be earned or purchased. It is not by church membership, by sacraments, by works, by law, or by the acts of any human being. It is not something which can be bestowed by a priest or preacher.

To the Baptist salvation is the work of the Holy Spirit in the human heart when an individual personally repents of sin and believes in the Lord Jesus as his Savior. In that moment the Spirit cleanses from sin's curse and gives the believer a new nature. "If any man be in Christ, he is a new creature" (2 Cor. 5:17). It is an individual experience, it is a personal experience, and it is a spiritual experience. This is why the Baptist asks, "Are you saved?"

Dr. Buell Kazee says, "Baptists believe that all who repent toward God and put their faith in the Lord Jesus Christ are saved, anywhere, everywhere, under any condition, without church membership, without baptism, in any church or denomination, or with any kind of baptism."

5. This salvation is everlasting. It is eternal life which God gives. Eternal life is not something one can have today, and then lose tomorrow. When a person believes unto salvation, he is saved forever. He becomes a child of God, and never can cease to be God's child. The Bible says that God promises eternal life, and gives it. God holds the believer in his hands, he does the keeping, and nothing in earth, hell, or heaven can separate him from the love of God which he has in Christ Jesus. How precious are the words of our Lord in John 10:27–29 "My sheep hear my voice, and I know them, and they follow me: And I give unto them eternal life; and they shall never perish, neither shall any man pluck them out of my hand. My Father, which gave them me, is greater than all, and no man is able to pluck them out of my Father's hand." With Christ's promise like that, how could the devil get one of God's children? With Paul, Baptists say, "For I am persuaded, that neither death, nor life, nor angels, nor principalities, nor powers, nor things present, nor things to come, nor height, nor depth, nor any other creature, shall be able to separate us from the love of God, which is in the Lord Jesus Christ" (Rom. 8:38–39).

6. This is a salvation which is for this life and for eternity. Paul

said, "For to me to live is Christ, and to die is gain" (Phil. 1:21). Salvation makes life new in this world. The saved person has the Holy Spirit living within him to help him live victoriously in this world and to have victory over death when that hour comes to him. This salvation provides life that reaches beyond the grave, to be spent eternally with the Lord in that place which he has prepared.

When the Baptist talks about being "saved" and about "eternal life" he is talking about both this life and the life to come.

After all, it would not be much salvation if it were only for this life, and it certainly would be incomplete if it were only for eternity.

Salvation is God's greatest gift to man. To Baptists the gospel which reveals it is the message above all other messages.

## THE CHURCH

The Baptist belief and emphasis concerning the New Testament church is one of the distinctives which differentiates them from other denominations.

What is a New Testament church?

A definition which probably is accepted by the majority of Baptists was set forth in the Statement of Faith adopted by the Southern Baptist Convention in 1963. That Statement says: "A New Testament church of the Lord Jesus Christ is a local body of baptized believers who are associated by covenant in the faith and fellowship of the gospel, observing the two ordinances of Christ, committed to his teaching, exercising the gifts, rights, and privileges invested in them by his word, and seeking to extend the gospel to the ends of the earth. This church is an autonomous body, operating through democratic processes under the lordship of Jesus Christ. In such a congregation, members are equally responsible. Its scriptural officers are pastors and deacons. The New Testament speaks also of the church as the body of Christ which includes all the redeemed of all ages."

1. This statement places its emphasis upon the church as "a

local body of baptized believers," but states that there also is a secondary meaning. Let us consider the Baptist position concerning the church as revealed in this statement.

(1) Baptists emphasize the church as a local body of baptized believers because this is the emphasis which is found in the New Testament. The Greek word *ekklesia,* translated "church" in the English Bible, is "used in the New Testament 114 times. Three times there clearly is no reference to the church. Eighty-five times the local idea is positively certain." In a number of other cases the reference clearly is generic or general, referring to the church as an institution. Three references appear to be speaking of an *ekklesia* in heaven, when all of the saved are together. There are references in ten verses in Ephesians and Colossians, where the apostle seems to be thinking of something other than the local church. It is largely from these that the larger or "universal" (theological term; not found in the Bible with reference to the church) concept of the church as the body of Christ made up of all the redeemed comes. However, many Baptist scholars interpret these passages as having the generic or institution meaning. Both Dr. B. H. Carroll and Dr. George W. McDaniel so classify them. Whatever may be one's interpretation, however, he must admit that in New Testament usage the primary emphasis is upon the "local" church.

This same emphasis is found in Jesus' use of the word. He spoke of the church twenty-three times, three in Matthew and nineteen in the book of Revelation. In every case except the first one, Matthew 16:18, he clearly is speaking of a "local" church. Matthew 16:18 is his declaration "Upon this rock I will build my church." Since every other reference is to the church as a local body, it seems reasonable to assume that Jesus had the same meaning here, except in an institutional sense. Nowhere did Jesus say that he would establish two kinds of churches, a local one and a universal one. It is because of this New Testament usage that Baptists give emphasis to the church as a local body.

(2) This church is to be made up of baptized believers. First, they must be "believers," by which Baptists mean that they must have been saved or born again. Unsaved persons may become members of Baptist churches, but they do so through a false or mistaken profession of faith. Second, these believers must be baptized, by which the Baptist means immersed. A New Testament church is, in Baptist thinking, a local, visible body made up of baptized believers. This is what is sometimes referred to as "a regenerate church membership." This belief immediately eliminates both infant baptism and any other type of church-related salvation.

(3) In Baptist belief and practice these churches are made up of baptized believers "associated by covenant in the faith and fellowship of the gospel, observing the ordinances, committed to his teaching, exercising the gifts, rights and privileges invested in them by his word. . . ." Here is a congregation of believers, worshiping together, working together, and, together seeking to do the Lord's will in all things.

(4) Each church is an autonomous body, completely independent, and in a democratic manner, administering its affairs under the headship of Jesus Christ. Baptists find in the New Testament no evidence of hierarchical or other type of outside control over the churches. New Testament churches elected deacons, sent out missionaries, exercised discipline, and carried on their work as a congregation. Baptists believe that they should have the same autonomy today. Cooperation with larger bodies such as associations or conventions, is entirely on a voluntary basis, and every Baptist church always is independent.

(5) In Baptist thinking, the church is the agency for carrying out Christ's commission to make disciples, baptize them, and teach them to observe all things which he had commanded. The church may do this independently, or it may cooperate with other churches of like faith and order in associations and conventions, in an enlarged program of witness. Most Baptist churches choose

to work in such denominational relationships, and the vast mission, educational, and benevolent programs being carried on by various Baptist groups today, are made possible through this voluntary cooperation of independent churches.

Baptist churches also usually cooperate with churches of other denominations in kingdom affairs, so long as that cooperation does not call for a sacrifice of doctrinal integrity or autonomy. In many areas such as morals, community uplift, social action, and others, Baptists always have worked with other groups. While some Baptists participate in the modern "ecumenical movements" feeling that there should be a Baptist voice in them, most Baptists have maintained a position apart from them, probably feeling with Dr. W. A. Criswell that "Ecumenicity is another name for death for our Baptist faith." Baptists so cherish their New Testament principles and their independence that they never are willing to relinquish them for mere outward unity. At the same time they count every person who accepts Jesus Christ as Lord and Savior as a brother, and always are ready to walk with him in kingdom affairs and fellowship, when no compromise is demanded or required.

Here then, is the New Testament church, as Baptists see it, believe concerning it, and emphasize it. It is a local body of baptized believers, seeking to carry out Christ's will here on the earth.

2. The Statement of Faith reveals that Baptists acknowledge that "The New Testament speaks also of the church as the body of Christ which includes all of the redeemed of all ages." It is interesting to note the change in Baptist emphasis in recent years, pointed up by the fact that this statement was not in the Statement of Faith adopted by Southern Baptists in 1925. There are two points of view concerning the meaning of this statement.

(1) To some Baptists it apparently means much the same that is meant by other denominations when they speak of the "body" of Christ, or of a "universal, invisible church." They believe that there is in existence now a "body" called the church, made up of all the saved on the earth, and that it is entered by the new birth.

Those holding this position believe that "local" churches are simply visible manifestations of the larger body.

(2) There are other Baptists who deny that there is actually a "universal, invisible church" in existence now, although probably most of them would agree that when all of the saved are together in heaven they will make one great "church" or assembly. They contend that there is nothing in the New Testament about people being "born again" into the church, and that proponents of this position are confusing it with the kingdom. They call attention to the fact that the words "universal" and "invisible" are never used concerning the church in the New Testament, and that the New Testament church always is an assembled or gathered group. A "universal" church could be only an ideal, since its membership could be known only to God, since it can have no meetings, no officers, and no program, and since it can be an actuality only when all of the redeemed are together in heaven. If someone argues that this breaks fellowship with all Christians other than Baptists, it is answered, "Not at all. They are in the kingdom, can be in local churches, and will be part of the true "universal" assembly gathered in glory. Here on earth, however, the church is local and visible."

Thus Baptists disagree concerning the meaning of church being something larger than a local, visible body, but they are generally agreed that the primary New Testament emphasis is on the local church, and it is to that body which they give their major attention.

## THE ORDINANCES

One cannot consider the Baptist distinctives, without looking at their teachings concerning the ordinances. Perhaps no doctrines held by Baptists set them apart from others as much as these. Baptists believe that the New Testament teaches two ordinances: the initial one, baptism, and the recurring one, the Lord's Supper, in that order.

No teachings of the New Testament have, in the thinking of Baptists, been more erroneously interpreted, or have been the basis of more false teaching, than the ordinances. Baptists reject all interpretations which make them sacramental in character, believing that rather than being procurative (of salvation) in their nature, they simply proclaim great gospel truths. Baptists believe that the ordinances have no part either in procuring salvation, in retaining it, or in adding anything to it. Rather, they proclaim what Christ has done for man is saving him, and serve as a memorial of that glorious act of God in providing redemption for man. Let us consider the two ordinances separately:

## BAPTISM

Baptism is the initial ordinance. The first command concerning the Christian after his salvation is that he be baptized. Our Lord, in his commission to his churches commanded them to make disciples, baptize them and then teach them to observe all things the Lord has commanded.

Baptists look upon baptism as a proclamation of Christ's death, burial and resurrection, and of the believer's death to sin, burial with Christ, and resurrection to a new life. Paul so describes baptism in Romans 6:1–3. He also describes baptism as an act in which we "put on Christ" (Gal. 3:27). Dr. A. T. Robertson says "put on" means "as a badge or uniform of service as that of a soldier." The uniform does not make a man a soldier, but proclaims to the world that he is one. Baptism, to the Baptist, has nothing to do with making a person a Christian, but when a person is baptized it is proclaimed to the world that he is a Christian.

Baptists believe the New Testament teaches that baptism is for believers only. They find no basis in the Scriptures either for infant baptism or baptism of any other person who has not professed faith in Christ. Household baptisms are mentioned but there is not the slightest evidence that there were infants in them. Every baptism mentioned is of believers.

This baptism of believers was by immersion. Sprinkling and

pouring, as related to baptism, are not even mentioned in the New Testament. Moreover, the Greek word *baptizo,* (baptize) always means to dip, plunge or immerse. Furthermore, the New Testament says that when people were baptized they went "down into the water," were "buried" in water, and "came up out of the water." Finally, our Lord walked sixty miles to be immersed of John the Baptist in the Jordan River, and a voice from heaven said, "This is my beloved Son in whom I am well pleased." That settles the matter for the Baptist. Baptism is the immersion of a believer in water, by the church, upon his profession of faith in Christ.

Their understanding of the New Testament teaching concerning baptism leads Baptists to reject the doctrine of baptismal regeneration, which means that baptism is essential for salvation, and that a child or an adult becomes a child of God when he is "baptized." Baptists see regeneration as a spiritual experience, wrought in the heart of the individual by the Holy Spirit when that person repents of sin and believes in the Lord Jesus Christ as his personal Savior. Neither baptism nor any other rite has anything to do with it, in Baptist thinking.

Baptists also reject the baptismal practices of sprinkling and pouring and the baptism of infants, all of which evidently came from the doctrine of "baptismal regeneration." Baptists are shocked and grieved when they think of how many people in the world may be lost because they may have been led to believe that they were made children of God by a rite of "baptism," and are depending upon that for salvation.

There is disagreement among Baptists as to what the term "baptized believer" means, so that some Baptist churches accept immersions from other denominations. However, a large percentage of them still reject all baptisms except those which they feel meet the four requirements for scriptural baptism: proper subject, a believer; proper form, immersion; proper purpose, to proclaim salvation, not to procure it; and proper authority, a New Testament church.

Baptists believe that while baptism is not essential for salvation, it still is of utmost importance, both because the Lord commanded it, and because it was the practice of the New Testament churches. They do not believe that any command of the Lord or New Testament practice can be ignored today.

## THE LORD'S SUPPER

The second ordinance, the recurring one, is the Lord's Supper. Baptists are generally agreed on its meaning, although they do not fully agree on the manner of its observance.

They are practically universally agreed on the meaning of the Lord's Supper. To them it is a memorial, and they reject all interpretations that it is a sacrament or has anything to do with securing or maintaining salvation.

Baptists are familiar with the Roman Catholic teaching of transubstantiation in which it is taught that in the observance (the mass) the bread and wine become the actual flesh and blood of Christ and are sacramental or saving. They know, too, of the Lutheran doctrine of consubstantiation, which says that the body and blood of Christ are present in the observance. They also know of the teachings of some others that there is some type of mystical presence and so some spiritual blessing in the observance or that it even is necessary for salvation. Baptists do not accept any of these interpretations, finding no ground for them in the Bible.

To the Baptist the Lord's Supper is a memorial. As the church observes the memorial, it is pointing back to the death, burial, and resurrection of Christ, but also is looking forward to his return. "This do in remembrance of me" said our Lord (1 Cor. 11:24). He also said, "For as often as ye eat this bread and drink this cup, ye do shew the Lord's death till he come" (1 Cor. 11:26). What a memorial this is, the only one that our Lord gave! No monuments, no buildings, just this simple memorial, "This do in remembrance of me."

While Baptists fully agree on the meaning and purpose of the Lord's Supper, they disagree on the manner of observing it.

Through their history Baptists have generally been known as "close communionists," meaning that the Lord's Supper was observed by Baptists in their churches without inviting other Christians to participate. Actually it was not "close communion" but really should have been called "close baptism" since it was the teaching on baptism which determined who would participate in the Lord's Supper. Baptists, along with almost all denominations, believe that only baptized persons have a right to come to the Lord's table, so, since they rejected anything as baptism except the "immersion of believers" for the proper purpose and under the proper authority, Baptists simply did not invite to the Lord's table those whom they did not believe had had scriptural baptism.

Some Baptist churches of today, however, have moved into the "open communion" position, making it more of a Christian ordinance than a church ordinance. Still others simply observe the Lord's Supper in a church service without defining who shall participate.

Other Baptists believe that "open communion" is impossible. They base that belief upon Paul's statement earlier in this eleventh chapter of 1 Corinthians, where he says that he understands that there are "divisions" and "heresies" (false teachings) in the Corinthian church, and since this is true, "When ye come together . . . this is not to eat the Lord's Supper" (1 Cor. 11:20). Accordingly, if there are divisions either in fellowship or doctrine, the supper is "not" the Lord's Supper. Not every Baptist accepts this interpretation, but many believe this is the clear meaning of the verse.

To most Baptists, the memorial supper is to be observed by the church assembled. It is not a denominational ordinance and among most Baptists is not observed at denominational meetings. Neither do most of them feel that it is a sacrament to be carried into homes to be ministered to individuals. They feel that only as the church assembles for the purpose of remembering the Lord can it be observed. Some Baptists believe that participation should be limited to the membership of the local church observing the ordinance, but probably most Baptist churches invite other Baptists to participate.

These, then, as Baptists see them, are the two ordinances which the Lord gave to his churches. They stand forever as great symbols of some of the central truths of the Christian faith.

## A PRINCIPLE

One of the marks of Baptists is their belief in the absolute separation of church and state.

Dr. Frank S. Mead says concerning Baptists: "Complete separation of church and state! They have never been a state church, have never taken orders from any government or king; in their blood is an eternal insistence that the State shall rule only in affairs political and let the Church alone. They are God's patriots, putting allegiance to him always above allegiance to Caesar. Freedom of conscience and complete divorce of church and state. How they have suffered for that! They have faced mockery and mud, fines, whippings, and iron bars; they have been burned at the stakes and pulled at the rack, but they have held to it. Their torturers might as well have expected man to walk without a head as to expect to tear that out of the Baptist. And note this and remember it: never once in their bitter, bloody history have they struck back at their persecutors, or persecuted any other for his faith. This is patriotism touched by the divine."

Dr. George W. Truett loved to preach of this glorious principle of religious liberty and separation of church and state. In his book *God's Call to America* he says, "We shall do well, both as citizens and as Christians, if we will hark back to the chief actors and lessons in the early and epoch-making struggles of this great Western democracy, for the full establishment of civil and religious liberty—back to the days of Washington and Jefferson and Madison, and back to the days of our Baptist fathers, who have paid such a great price, through the long generations, that liberty, both religious and civil, might have free course and be glorified everywhere.

"Years ago, at a notable dinner in London, that world-famed statesman, John Bright, asked an American statesman, himself a Baptist, the noble Dr. J. L. M. Curry, 'What distinct contribution has your America made to the science of government?' To that question Dr. Curry replied: 'The doctrine of religious liberty.' After a moment's reflection, Mr. Bright made the worthy reply: 'It was a tremendous contribution.' "

Dr. Truett adds "The impartial historian, whether in the past, present, or future, will ever agree with our American historian, Mr. Bancroft, when he says, 'Freedom of conscience, unlimited freedom of mind, was from the first the trophy of Baptists.' "

The Baptist wants freedom for himself and his churches.

He wants the same freedom for all other men.

He ever has opposed the state church, or state support of the church, his own, or any other.

Not religious toleration! The Baptist does not believe in that. That states that someone else has the right to tolerate you. Baptists reject that. They believe that they are right in doctrine, but they claim no right to judge others. Their position is religious liberty for all men.

They believe, too, that every man is responsible to God alone.

One of the curses of the "Christian" world, in Baptist thinking, has been the uniting of church and state. Some countries in Europe, have a state church, with church expenses paid by the government. While America does not have such a situation, there is a continuous effort on the part of some to secure tax funds for church-controlled institutions. Baptists have opposed this throughout their history and they are opposing it today. Their call is for a free church in a free state, with every man free to worship God as he will, or will not.

This is the Baptist position. It is what Baptists believe the Bible teaches.

## A PROGRAM

One of the reasons many people are Baptists and remain Baptists is because of the program of work carried out by Baptists in their churches.

What is the program of a New Testament church? What are churches supposed to do?

As one examines the whole realm of Christianity, he finds programs that are varied. Some churches have become little more than social agencies, doing the work of good will centers, community centers, and the like. Others are much like social clubs. It is rather shocking to hear of dancing, bingo parties, and similar social activities in modern church buildings. Some churches become deeply involved in political action, and other become mere business concerns, competing with the world. But are these actually the fields of action where New Testament churches should be spending their energies?

Most Baptists think not, and as one examines Baptist churches closely, he finds that whether they are large or small, rural or urban, rich or poor, basically they have a general agreement upon the major tasks they believe God has given them. These tasks are based upon the Great Commission of our Lord. "Go ye therefore, and teach [make disciples of] all nations, baptizing them in the name of the Father, and of the Son, and of the Holy Ghost: teaching them to observe all things whatsoever I have commanded you, and lo, I am with you alway, even unto the end of the age" (Matt. 28:19–20). To the Baptist these are the marching orders of the church.

Certainly, it is out of this commission that Baptist churches have built their program. What is that program?

1. Baptists believe that the first task of the church is to evangelize. Go "make disciples" said Jesus. That is evangelism. It is the central task of the church. We already have seen that Baptists believe that every man is lost and needs to be saved. To them being

"saved" or "born again" is the most important matter in life and they center their program upon it.

Baptists preach the gospel to win men to Christ. They build Sunday Schools to win people to the Lord. They hold revivals to reach the lost about them. They train witnesses to bring the lost to the Savior. They pray for God's power and direction in leading the unsaved to a new birth in Jesus Christ.

If you visit a Baptist church auditorium or sanctuary, almost always you will find the pulpit in the center. This is because Baptists believe that the preaching of the gospel is to be central to all they do. They hear the words of the Bible that it is "by the foolishness of preaching" that men are brought to repentance and faith.

The word evangelize becomes a flaming word to most Baptists, and to many Christians this is one of the most attractive characteristics of Baptists. They are evangelistic.

2. Baptists also major on missions. Their concern about evangelism makes them missionary in their program. They believe that the command of Christ is to carry the message of salvation to the whole world. They believe that there is "none other name . . . given among men, whereby we must be saved" (Acts 4:12), and that all people of the world are lost without Jesus Christ. They reject the idea that Christianity is just another religion in the midst of all the religions of the world. They believe that it stands alone, and that men must come to Christ if they are to be saved. This has made Baptists missionary in their concern.

This missionary concern has sent them into all the world. They begin with local missions in the areas around them. Then they reach beyond the home community to associational missions, state missions, home missions for all of their native land, and foreign missions that reaches out to nations beyond. It would be difficult to find a point in the world where missionaries from some Baptist group have not touched. As one reads the records of Christian world missions, he finds at the top of the lists, some of the greatest missionary leaders, men like William Carey, Adoniram Judson, and Luther Rice. In modern mission work, few groups, if any, are ahead of Baptists. Missions is the very heartbeat of the churches and the denominations. Indeed it was missions that caused the formation of Baptist denominational groups, and it still is missions that holds them together. This missionary zeal and missionary program inspires and challenges many Baptists so that they want to be a part of it.

3. Education. A third division of Baptist work is education—Christian education. Baptists believe that the part of the Great Commission concerning teaching should be a positive part of the work of every church. This Christian education begins in the home, where Baptists are urged to teach their children the great truths of the Word of God. It continues in the church through the Sunday School and other organizations. No denomination has used the Sunday School more effectively than some Baptist groups. The Sunday School is more than a teaching agency since it finds people, brings them under the influence of the church, leads many of them to Christ, and then helps them grow in the Christian life, yet its primary purpose is teaching, teaching the Word of God. The Bible is still the textbook in Baptist Sunday Schools and while literature is used, it always is for the purpose of helping understand the text, the Bible itself. Baptists also use other teaching organizations as Church Training, the Vacation Bible Schools, and the Mission organizations.

Baptist educational concern, however, reaches far beyond the church doors. They were among the first to see the need for Christian institutions of higher learning and some of the first colleges in America were founded by Baptists. Today, no denomination in America surpasses Baptists in the number of colleges, universities, or seminaries established and supported. Around the world Baptists have such institutions. Furthermore, Baptists have established a program of student ministries which reaches on to almost every campus in America. The largest Christian seminaries in America are Baptist. Christian education is a basic part of the program of world missions supported by Baptist groups. Baptists believe in Christian education.

4. Other ministries. It would be impossible, in space as limited as we have here, to name all of the other ministries of Baptists. We must list a few of them. There is a great hospital ministry which has provided some of the finest healing institutions in the world; there are children's homes, which care for literally thousands of children from broken or no longer existing homes. There is a ministry to the older people, the senior citizens. Baptists long have been in the field of social action and have increased their emphasis on it in recent years. There are ministries in the area of morals and civic affairs. There are ministries to servicemen, largely through the chaplaincy. We could go on and on. Baptists are activists in many areas, and some people love the Baptists and remain with them because of their program.

# SECTION IV

## Baptist Devotion to Doctrine and Truth

### A Message by J. D. Grey

## "BAPTIST DEVOTION TO DOCTRINE AND TRUTH"

(This sermon was preached by Dr. J. D. Grey, pastor of the First Baptist Church, New Orleans, Louisiana, in his own pulpit at the morning service on Sunday, June 8, 1969, just before the opening of the Southern Baptist Convention held in New Orleans the following week. Hundreds of visitors were present in the congregation. The house was packed to its utmost capacity. This sermon was mechanically recorded and is now being reproduced, with only slight abridgement. This is a sermon concerning Southern Baptists but the principles apply to all Baptists.)

The 119th Psalm and 63rd verse has been a great inspiration to me. "I am a companion of all them that fear thee and of them that keep thy precepts." Baptists have been known through their long history and distinguished by their loyalty to the Word of God. Traditionally they have been a people of the Book. In that regard they are like the children of Israel who answered Moses according to Exodus 24:7, "All that the Lord hath said we will do, and be obedient." It goes without saying, of course, that all Baptists everywhere at all times do not follow that exactly, but it is the sentiment of Baptists that we will follow all that the Lord hath said to us and in it to be obedient. We take literally the words of the apostle Peter as recorded in Acts 5:29, "We ought to obey God rather than men." This devotion to the doctrines of the Word of God is one explanation for the blessings that God has given to them, one explanation for the blessings that have been showered upon them as they have sought to honor the Lord and stay true to his Word.

This day in which we live, beloved brothers and sisters, is no day for dillydallying, or shillyshalling, by mealymouthed preachers. It is the day of all days for no stammerer in the pulpit or an insipid, spineless, and convictionless Christian in the pew. And if we are to continue our contributions to Kingdom progress for the glory of God, we must hold convictions about the teachings of the Word of God as deep as life itself. The absence of convictions about the Word of God will result in an anemic denomination, an insipid church, and spineless church members who are lacking in character, in stamina, and in enthusiasm. Therefore, this morning I direct your thoughts to the theme: "Baptist Devotion to Truth."

## I

I begin by suggesting that first of all, gratitude to our Baptist forebears elicits our devotion to truth and to doctrine. Gratitude to those who have been our progenitors, those who have bequeathed unto us legacies as great as life itself. Ours is a noble heritage in martyrdom that has been left to us by those who suffered for the faith before us. To paraphrase the words of the apostle Paul, "With a great price obtained we our freedom." Baptists have been hated and persecuted for centuries even back to the days of the despised Anabaptists, and even before that. Emperor Charles V issued an edict against them at Brussels on June 10, 1535, which said in part that "those who have rebaptized any person or who have borne or had the name of prophet, apostles, or bishops shall be put to death by fire." Many of the ancestors of ours were in that group that suffered.

Martin Luther, the father of the Reformation, left us a great heritage in many ways. I have often said "he went out the front door of the Catholic Church, but he didn't go off the front steps." Martin Luther even anathematized the Baptists of his time because they taught that infants could be saved without infant baptism. In 1525 at Zurich, Switzerland, Zwingli, the co-reformer of Luther and Calvin had several public debates with the Baptists on the question of "infant baptism." His followers claimed the victory and proceeded to put the Baptists in prison.

In England John Bunyan of literary and spiritual fame was imprisoned twelve long years at Bedford because King Charles II of England forbade him to preach the gospel. One day some representatives of the king came and said to Bunyan, "If you will promise to cease and desist from preaching in the public squares and preaching publicly the king has said you will have amnesty, we will not put you in prison." And old John Bunyan said, "Tell the king if he lets me out of prison this morning, I'll be at Elstow in the square preaching the gospel before sundown."

That's the kind of stock we Baptists came of, and aren't we ashamed of ourselves when we weaken our position, apologize for it, and compromise it for expediency sake. When our forebears came to the New World it was not much better. They were relentlessly persecuted by other religious groups. It is a well-known fact in history that a law was passed in the Colony in Massachusetts in 1644 banishing Baptists because they rejected infant baptism and would not yield to the established church, which in that case was the Congregational faith. Roger Williams was banished from Massachusetts for his Baptist sentiments and later established Providence, Rhode Island Colony, the first place where religious freedom was granted upon the face of God's green earth.

Pursuant to the edict of 1644 about preaching the gospel Obadiah Holmes who resisted it went on to the Boston Commons to preach the gospel. He was publicly whipped in Boston Commons until blood ran down to his ankles. When he stumbled away in weakness from being thus punished for preaching the gospel, he said, "It was as though they had struck me with roses." Then in the neighboring state of Connecticut a Baptist preacher was put in stocks for "preaching the gospel contrary to the law." In Georgia a Baptist preacher was jailed because he preached the gospel without a permit from the Episcopal Bishop. Henry Dunster, the first president of Harvard College, was forced to resign after serving with distinction for fifteen years because he opposed their views on infant baptism. In 1768 in Spottsylvania County in Virginia three Baptist preachers were dragged before the magistrate for trial. The renowned Patrick Henry voluntarily defended them, waving the indictment before the magistrates and repeating it and again and again reading it saying, "For preaching the gospel of the Son of God—great God, man, do you mean to tell me men are put in jail for preaching the gospel of the matchless Son of

God." And a score of these same Baptist preachers languished in prison at Culpepper jail for the same charge because they preached the gospel without a permit from the Episcopal authorities.

Through the centuries until this day even in recent times when William Wallace, our noble Baptist missionary was martyred in China to the Communists, Baptists have suffered for their faith. No spineless, no anemic, no compromising group of Christians were these who were our spiritual forerunners. I say, therefore, gratitude to our forebears should give us a devotion to truth.

II

Furthermore, our belief in the Bible as our only rule of faith and practice certainly necessitates a devotion to doctrine and to truth. I have seen preachers come and go in this town. I have heard their laments of attendance dwindling away, not just in summertime, but all the time, and I have inquired into what they have been preaching. Many of them have been reviewing books, many of them taking up the latest philosophy, taking up the various palliatives and the social gospel emphasis, and making their main emphasis relevance, which is a word I think today in many quarters is already overworked.

The gospel has always been relevant, and men are sinners, they are lost, they are going to hell. We need to tell them how they can be saved, then tell them how they can love their neighbor, and how they can serve others, and how they can be decent and honorable and good citizens standing for what is right. But the message of the Word of God is our only rule of faith and practice. Every Baptist should vehemently declare, strongly assert and affirm, "God said it, I believe it, that settles it!"

That is exactly what the Lord was saying in the fifteenth chapter of Matthew when he gave a very sharp rebuke to his contemporaries in the ninth verse, "But in vain they do worship me, teaching for doctrines the commandments of men." Every one of us should agree with the sentiment of the great, noble, and illustrious George W. Truett who once said, "The encyclicals of councils and creeds, however ancient and venerable, cannot take the place of one clear, 'thus saith the Lord.' "

One clear "thus saith the Lord," and because the Bible is our only guide, we must be Bible-loving, Bible-reading, Bible-believing, Bible-teaching, and Bible-obeying people. Our children in the earlier years are taught so much about the bees and the birds and the flowers and all of that until the time runs out before they have a chance to tell them that God made it all. I guess I am old-fashioned and corny and country. But I was brought up in the card class in the country Sunday School up in Kentucky. I'll tell you right now, those lessons those teachers taught us off the little ole card with the picture of Jesus blessing the children, I'll never get away from them. I think a lot more of them than if they had taught me how to build a bird's nest, or something like that.

Harry Rimmer one time said during a revival in this church some years ago, "I love you Baptists— (you know he was a Presbyterian)—and admire you because Baptists believe the Bible, Baptists are devoted to the Bible, Baptists will die for the Bible, Baptists will do anything but read the Bible." You and I should never be ashamed of the teachings that we derive from the Word of God and not hesitate to declare them at all times, in all places, under all circumstances. I don't mean just organizing little study courses off in little dark rooms in a corner two or three nights a week. I mean enunciating them from the pulpit, on the radio and television, so others may know what the Word of God says.

III

I say furthermore that our devotion to truth requires building a wall of truth around our people. We need to indoctrinate our people so that they will not be carried away with every wind of doctrine that comes along as Paul warned us by inspiration in Ephesians 4:14. We must protect our people. The apostle Paul said much to the preachers in the New Testament when he advised that we are the shepherds of the flock, and the shepherd is to defend the sheep. Of course he is to doctor the sheep and he is to shear the sheep, but he is also to protect the sheep, he is to feed the sheep, and he is to strengthen the sheep. Because you know today there are many vagaries of religious teachers whose great forte is breaking into sheepfolds and being sheep-stealers. There are some sects and some groups that are like leeches that live by misleading the weak and uninformed members of our churches. I have a personal indictment against myself every time intelligence comes to me that there has been a defection on the part of one of our members, whose name is dropped from our roll because he has gone to another faith. Where did I fail? Where did we fail in teaching him the Word of God? The Bible plainly warns us that in the latter times there will be many false teachers that will arise and that people will be led away from the truth. Therefore, I say to build a wall of truth about our people.

Paul dwelt on this and by inspiration, he said in 2 Timothy 4:3–4: "For the time will come when they will not endure sound doctrine; but after their own lusts shall they heap to themselves teachers, having itching ears; and they shall turn away their ears from the truth, and shall be turned unto fables." We have certainly come upon times described by that. When the truth of the Bible is taught, all error will be exposed and opposed. I say we need today to have courses in apologetics and polemics in our colleges and seminaries for our young preachers so they may *know* how to analyze error, answer error, expose error, and deal with error. We need a new emphasis upon "contending earnestly for the faith." Yes, contend without becoming contentious, remembering the words of Ephesians 4:15, "speaking the truth in love."

IV

There is another consideration—adherence to our democratic idealism certainly evokes a devotion to truth. Through the centuries human freedom has been a cardinal tenet with Baptists, not simply when they were a minority, but also when they were a majority, for others as well as for themselves. The other day I taped our nine o'clock broadcast on the Gospel Hour which was heard on WNOE at 9:00 this morning. We've been on that station for over thirty years, broadcasting the Gospel Hour every Sunday morning. I preached this morning on "Baptists and Individualism." I wanted our friends and neighbors reached by WNOE, a 50,000 watt daytime station, to know what we Baptists believe and why we believe it. I bore down on the point that we have always fought for the freedom of others, as well as for ourselves. Roger Williams founded the first Baptist church in America at Providence, Rhode Island. He also founded the first commonwealth on earth in which there was absolute civil and religious liberty. Bancroft, the noted historian, said, "Freedom of conscience, unlimited freedom of mind, was from the first the trophy of the Baptists." I get rather sick and tired of all this self-styled intellectual idiocy when people look down their egotistical noses at Baptists as though we were a bunch of red-necks and backwoodsmen that never did anything except raise Cain and try to close up a liquor store. We've done all these things, yes—somebody needs to raise some Cain and some things stronger than that in these cities and in other places. We need to continue to do it, but I tell you through the years Baptists have been advocates of freedom of conscience. This government under which we live was formed and fashioned upon the model of a Baptist church. I say that without fear of any contradiction. Thomas Jefferson frequently attended a little Baptist church near Monticello, Virginia of which Rev. Andrew Tribble was the pastor. Mr. Jefferson was often witness to the congregation transacting its business. He was very much impressed with the manner in which they did this in a democratic fashion, and he concluded that their plan of government would be the best possible plan for the American colony. I say that upon no less authority than Mrs. James Madison who wrote, "Mr. Jefferson *did* gather those views from a Baptist church."

The article on religious liberty, the First Amendment to the Constitution in the Bill of Rights, was put in there largely through the united and insistent efforts of the Baptists of Virginia. After the Constitution was promulgated and sent out for ratification by the thirteen colonies, the Baptists of Virginia said to James Monroe, James Madison, Thomas Jefferson, and others: "We will be for it, but you must put in there an article on religious liberty." John Leland and others were successful in getting the First Amendment dealing with religious liberty and other liberties put into our Constitution.

You and I need today a holy rededication to our "doctrine of the democracy of the saints" as our late and great leader M. E. Dodd used to call it. We preach and fight for political freedom in opposition to dictatorships. We *must* favor just as strongly soul freedom from all forms of ecclesiastical absolutism. As we oppose despotism in politics we must oppose absolutism in spiritual matters. Our devotion to the doctrine of democracy will make us in conscience sake oppose every move to destroy or to weaken religious freedom. We as Baptists must continue to advocate the complete separation of church and state as guaranteed in our Bill of Rights, thus saving America from that curse that has come upon other nations where church and state have been united in unholy wedlock and human freedoms have soon perished.

V

Furthermore maintaining our denominational solidarity calls for a devotion to doctrine and for devotion to truth: Only as Southern Baptists are loyal to our Lord and his Word can we maintain a solid front. We will become fragmented and divided when everyone goes as a law unto himself. We must stay with the Word of God. The genius of our program at home and abroad has made us the marvel of many and the envy of some. This is explained only by the fact that we have stayed "together in fellowship and in the apostles' doctrine" and in the labors of the Lord Jesus Christ. God's rich blessings have been upon our labors as a denomination as they have in such a way as to make us grateful and to make us humble. Some years ago a study was made of fifteen leading denominations and it showed that in a twenty-five-year span beginning in 1925 Southern Baptists had increased in members and in gifts above all the others. In that twenty-five-year span Southern Baptists had increased 67 percent in members while the other denominations had increased only 36 percent. Also our gifts had increased 319 percent while the average increase among the other denominations was only 80 percent. I believe we Southern Baptists still have a message and still need to give it. Our devotion to the truth of God has unified us for conquest.

How can one explain the way in which the eleven million plus members in our thirty-four thousand plus cooperating Southern Baptist churches can maintain a solidarity in service without any visible head or ecclesiastical overlordship? Our cohesiveness and our unswerving loyalty to our common Lord and to the Word of God has made no ecclesiastical hierarchy and overlordship at all necessary. Furthermore, these are repugnant to Baptist thought. "All ye are brethren and one is your Lord." It will be a sad day when the Southern Baptist Convention usurps the prerogatives of the local churches and presumes to dictate to them in any manner of doctrine or practice. It can recommend and suggest, but that's all. The churches must remain free to cooperate as they choose. The rule has been and must ever be "cooperation always—coercion never." Maintaining of our solidarity, our dedication to a separation, demands a devotion to truth.

## VI

Furthermore our expanding evangelism compels a devotion to truth. A wholesome and an abiding evangelism must be rooted and grounded in the deep truths of God's Word. A doctrineless evangelism and a bloodless social gospel alike will cause us to build upon sand instead of upon the solid rock of the Word of God. We must build upon the Word. We cite three of many truly great evangelistic churches in America that were built by mighty men of God who had a hot heart, were evangelistic, and yet had a solid doctrinal foundation. I nominate these three yet many others could be named. I mention these three because I know more intimately about these three that have stood through the years than perhaps any others. The First Baptist Church of Shreveport, pastored by M. E. Dodd for thirty-eight years, is devoted to the truth of the Word of God and yet is evangelistic. The great First Baptist Church of Minneapolis, Minnesota, where the late William B. Riley worked in mighty labors for the Lord for forty-four years. The Bellevue Baptist Church of Memphis where the inimitable Robert Greene Lee was pastor for thirty-three years. He has preached and preached the Bible and baptized thousands. I resent the idea that doctrinal preaching and an evangelistic ministry are divorced. They can and should go together. Evangelistic preaching that would bring permanent results must be firmly rooted in the cardinal doctrines of the Bible, the doctrine of sin, of judgment, of hell, of repentance, of atonement, of security of the believer, the doctrine of the church and of its ordinances, of baptism and the Lord's Supper. These pleasing palliatives which preach only the love of God will never bring the lasting results.

One thing about Billy Graham's preaching that I love is when I hear him say, "The Bible says, the Bible says, the Bible says." He repeats that almost to the point of being tedious and repetitious but his evangelism is rooted in the Word of God. We must have a revival of preaching of hellfire and brimstone to arouse the anesthetized consciences of sinners who have wronged the Holy God.

For the thirty-two years that I have walked in the main marts of trade and business activity in this city and on the streets of this city, I have "shunned not to declare the whole counsel of God" unto them. I have said to crooked public officials and I am saying it this week, and I said it last week, "You are corrupt and need to get these things straightened out." Yet underneath it all, basically is that men need God in their hearts and lives. In the conditions of crime and so on that plague our country, the remedies are effective for the eradication of them are good as far as they go. But until we redeem the soul of the individual and bring him to repentance and faith, we are just bailing water out of a boat that has a hole in it that is letting more in than we are able to bail out, and it is sinking fast. When we have been won to repentance and faith for salvation we should lead others to come to the baptismal waters in obedience, in church membership. A revival that doesn't wind up with a baptizing is not much of a revival.

## VII

Our devotion to truth will lead us to teach them to observe all things whatsoever Christ has demanded us. That was a great day when William Carey had his first convert. He worked for six and a half years to translate the New Testament into Bengali. On March 5, 1801, when he translated the Bible into Bengali and laid it on the Lord's Supper table in that church, it is said he laid the axe of God's truth at the root of the Banyan tree of error, mysticism, Hinduism, and the other isms that had plagued India. He did it by his translation of the New Testament into the Bengali language.

I tell this story often—many in this church have heard me give it—but I close with it today. I think it is so appropriate as a challenge to my own people and a challenge to you who are not even Baptists. Against this backdrop that I have tried to place this morning I wanted to interpret what you will be hearing on television and radio and reading in the newspapers about these Southern Baptists who gather here this week. Ours is an ongoing program. We have great emphases that we will make on convictions we hold. We have commitments that must be renewed. I tell this story that comes from antiquity and from the very classic of literature, Xenophon's *Anabasis*.

The Greeks had been fighting in far-off Persia two thousand miles from home without supplies, without reinforcements. They had been harassed by the enemy. When they started back home to Greece across the hot sands of the desert, and the snows of the mountains, and the streams, they kept on their way back. It was described when Xenophon in his *Anabasis* uses two Greek words above all others, *Entythen Exelauni,* which literally mean "from there we went on." They tell about their battles and "from there we went on," about their hardships here and privations there and their need for food and still "from there we went on."

We Southern Baptists must continue to view our position and say, "From there we went on."